Mastering Apple Aperture

Master the art of enhancing, organizing, exporting, and printing your photos using Apple Aperture

Thomas Fitzgerald

PUBLISHING

BIRMINGHAM - MUMBAI

Mastering Apple Aperture

First published: August 2013

Production Reference: 1200813

Published by Packt Publishing Ltd.
Livery Place
35 Livery Street
Birmingham B3 2PB, UK.

ISBN 978-1-84969-356-1

www.packtpub.com

Cover Image by Thomas Fitzgerald (thomasfitzgerald@mac.com)

Credits

Author
Thomas Fitzgerald

Reviewers
Chris Jones
Daniel Schildt
Ryan Valle

Acquisition Editor
Kunal Parikh

Lead Technical Editor
Neeshma Ramakrishnan

Technical Editors
Kapil Hemnani
Akashdeep Kundu
Sonali S. Vernekar

Project Coordinator
Apeksha Chitnis

Proofreader
Joanna McMahon

Indexer
Tejal Soni

Graphics
Ronak Dhruv

Production Coordinator
Pooja Chiplunkar

Cover Work
Pooja Chiplunkar

About the Author

Thomas Fitzgerald has been trained in animation and graphic designing, and from there he became a motion graphics artist working in television and film, but he always pursued his love for photography. His work with the visual medium of motion pictures encouraged his skills as a photographer and his cross-disciplined approach led him to his passion for photography today. Currently, Thomas is a freelance motion graphics artist and animator, as well as a fine art photographer and a prolific blogger. He has been using Aperture since the very first version came out, and writes and produces a popular blog about Aperture, http://theapertureblog.com.

I wish to thank my wonderful wife Mary, without whom I doubt this book would have ever been written. She has encouraged and helped me at every step and without her support you would not be reading this book today. I also want to thank my Dad without whom I doubt I would have ever developed a love for photography. My father was a keen photographer, and cameras, enlargers, lenses, and darkroom chemicals always surrounded me growing up. One of the earliest memories I have from childhood is of the line of beautifully photographed black and white portraits of our family that hung in the long hallway of our first house. I believe this inspired my love of photography from an early age. I want to thank the rest of my family who have helped encourage my artistic tendencies over the years and especially my mother for all the love and support she has given me.

Finally, I want to thank my good friends Michael, Eugene, Ian, and Gergo for their friendship and support.

About the Reviewers

Chris Jones is a programmer by day, and became inspired to take up amateur photography by the arrival of his two children, who provide an almost endless supply of adorable moments that are nearly impossible to capture! His camera is an iPhone and he is trying very hard to work with its advantages and limitations, instead of getting sucked into the expensive world of DSLR cameras. Chris lives in London with Rike, Jasper, and Niklas.

Daniel Schildt has a background in visual communication, having studied photography, graphic design, video, and other types of tools at several schools. At the same time, his continuous interest in storytelling lead him to learning both art and technology. Recently he has worked on projects ranging from building 360 degree virtual tours to retouching photos for advertising. Currently he is learning data journalism. This is his first book project as a reviewer. He can be reached via Twitter @autiomaa and has a website at http://autiomaa.org.

Ryan Valle is a multimedia specialist with credited works in the areas of video, digital imaging, web development, and video games. Ryan earned a Bachelor of Arts degree in Multimedia Production in 2011 and over the years, has worked professionally in the areas of television and video production, photography, web design and development, and most recently, video games.

www.PacktPub.com

Support files, eBooks, discount offers, and more

You might want to visit www.PacktPub.com for support files and downloads related to your book.

Did you know that Packt offers eBook versions of every book published, with PDF and ePub files available? You can upgrade to the eBook version at www.PacktPub.com and as a print book customer, you are entitled to a discount on the eBook copy. Get in touch with us at service@packtpub.com for more details.

At www.PacktPub.com, you can also read a collection of free technical articles, sign up for a range of free newsletters and receive exclusive discounts and offers on Packt books and eBooks.

http://PacktLib.PacktPub.com

Do you need instant solutions to your IT questions? PacktLib is Packt's online digital book library. Here, you can access, read, and search across Packt's entire library of books.

Why Subscribe?

- Fully searchable across every book published by Packt
- Copy and paste, print and bookmark content
- On demand and accessible via web browser

Free Access for Packt account holders

If you have an account with Packt at www.PacktPub.com, you can use this to access PacktLib today and view nine entirely free books. Simply use your login credentials for immediate access.

Table of Contents

Preface

When Aperture first came out, there was nothing like it on the software front. There were tools for converting your raw photos and organizing your images, but none combined the two. I first started using Aperture almost immediately after it came out. It was not just a huge change in the way I went about managing my images, but the way I approached photography in general. It was a liberating experience and it meant that I spent less time managing folders and files, and more time enjoying the art.

Over the years, Apple has added more and more features to the software, and it has become more and more complex, yet it retains a high degree of approachability. But that ease of use hides a degree of complexity underneath the surface that makes it a powerful tool in the right hands.

It was the release of Aperture that led to a whole new class of photo management software and it is Aperture that is responsible for the phrase "photo workflow". Before Aperture, this concept didn't exist. Now, the model that Apple developed is pretty much the standard way to approach post production of digital photography, and while Aperture has attracted a number of competitors to the space, the software still has many unique features, especially if you dig beneath the surface. Digging beneath that surface is what I hope to achieve with this book.

The idea behind the book was simple; I wanted to approach it in a way that solves a problem that I personally have found with a lot of books written about software. You've probably run into this yourself. You know the basics of a piece of software and you want to increase your knowledge, but most training material is written with absolute beginners in mind. You end up going through a book and trying to sieve through the basic information that you already know, while searching for the nuggets of knowledge that are not just aimed at beginners. This can be so boring and tedious that one often gives up. On the other hand, you have books that are written for very advanced users that, while skipping out on the basics, also miss out much of the intermediate information that a person might want to know.

So, *Mastering Apple Aperture,* is aimed at the middle ground. It's for people who know the basics, but want to learn more. If you know how Aperture works, but you want to know more details and want to learn some of the not so obvious tips and tricks, then this book is for you. It is not a book for absolute beginners, as it was written with the assumption that you already know how to use Aperture a little bit. There are no boring explanations of how to install the software, how to use the menus, what each part of the interface is, and so on. Instead, this book will build on your existing knowledge of the software and help to turn you into a true master.

What this book covers

Chapter 1, Advanced Importing and Organizing, teaches the reader some of the advanced functionality of Aperture's import functionality, as well as techniques for organizing and sorting your library.

Chapter 2, Advanced Adjustments, introduces the reader to the theory behind how the camera RAW format works, and how to make use of Aperture's advanced image editing functionality.

Chapter 3, Everything You Ever Wanted to Know about Curves, takes an in-depth look at Aperture's curves tool as well as the theory behind curves and the histogram. You will learn how powerful feature the curves tool is and some of the many things you can do with it.

Chapter 4, Aperture in Action, builds on the previous chapters, and provides a set of real-world examples of how to use Aperture to complete various tasks.

Chapter 5, Extending Aperture, takes an in-depth look at Aperture's plugin architecture as well as looking at workflows for working with third-party software.

Chapter 6, Exporting and Outputting to the Web, looks at the many ways you can get your images out of Aperture and share them on social networks, photo sharing services or your own websites.

Chapter 7, Making Metadata Work for You, looks at the subject of metadata information, how to enter it, and how valuable it can be.

Chapter 8, Getting Better Prints from Aperture, looks at the subject of printing from Aperture, and how to get better quality and more accurate prints.

What you need for this book

This book is designed for people who are already familiar with the basics of
Aperture. It assumes you know how to use a computer, and more specifically a Mac.
It also assumes you have a copy of Aperture. This book was written for Aperture 3.4
or later version. If you have any version of Aperture 3, 3.4 is a free upgrade, but 3.3
and 3.4 added some key features that are covered in various parts of this book. It also
assumes you have a digital camera which can shoot in a RAW format and you have
access to RAW files.

Who this book is for

This book is designed for those who have a basic understanding of Aperture and
photography software in general. It is not designed for absolute beginners, and it
will not teach you the basics of using the software. You need to have a beginner's
level of experience with Aperture specifically, and photography software in general.
This book occasionally discusses photographic terms and concepts, so the reader
needs to have a basic understanding of photography and photographic theory.

Conventions

In this book, you will find a number of styles of text that distinguish between
different kinds of information. Here are some examples of these styles, and an
explanation of their meaning.

New terms and **important words** are shown in bold. Words that you see on
the screen, in menus or dialog boxes for example, appear in the text like this:
"Clicking on the **Next** button moves you to the next screen".

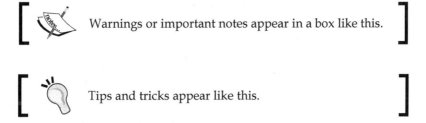

Warnings or important notes appear in a box like this.

Tips and tricks appear like this.

Downloading the color images of this book

We also provide you a PDF file that has color images of the screenshots/diagrams used in this book. The color images will help you better understand the changes in the output. You can download this file from `http://www.packtpub.com/sites/default/files/downloads/3561OT_ColorGraphics.pdf`.

Reader feedback

Feedback from our readers is always welcome. Let us know what you think about this book—what you liked or may have disliked. Reader feedback is important for us to develop titles that you really get the most out of.

To send us general feedback, simply send an e-mail to `feedback@packtpub.com`, and mention the book title via the subject of your message.

If there is a topic that you have expertise in and you are interested in either writing or contributing to a book, see our author guide on `www.packtpub.com/authors`.

Customer support

Now that you are the proud owner of a Packt book, we have a number of things to help you to get the most from your purchase.

Errata

Although we have taken every care to ensure the accuracy of our content, mistakes do happen. If you find a mistake in one of our books—maybe a mistake in the text or the code—we would be grateful if you would report this to us. By doing so, you can save other readers from frustration and help us improve subsequent versions of this book. If you find any errata, please report them by visiting `http://www.packtpub.com/submit-errata`, selecting your book, clicking on the **errata submission form** link, and entering the details of your errata. Once your errata are verified, your submission will be accepted and the errata will be uploaded on our website, or added to any list of existing errata, under the Errata section of that title. Any existing errata can be viewed by selecting your title from `http://www.packtpub.com/support`.

Piracy

Piracy of copyright material on the Internet is an ongoing problem across all media. At Packt, we take the protection of our copyright and licenses very seriously. If you come across any illegal copies of our works, in any form, on the Internet, please provide us with the location address or website name immediately so that we can pursue a remedy.

Please contact us at `copyright@packtpub.com` with a link to the suspected pirated material.

We appreciate your help in protecting our authors, and our ability to bring you valuable content.

Questions

You can contact us at `questions@packtpub.com` if you are having a problem with any aspect of the book, and we will do our best to address it.

1
Advanced Importing and Organizing

Importing and organizing your photographs are probably the two tasks that you perform most often in Aperture. Organizing your images within the software is a fundamental aspect of what Aperture does and a vital part of any photographer's workflow. Yet, surprisingly, this is an area that is often overlooked by many people who use this software. Novices and amateurs, in particular, are keen to learn how to process their images, but don't think how a few careful decisions at the import stage can make a huge difference to their workflow. The goal of this chapter is to look beyond the basics of importing and organizing. Even if you think you understand how to keep your photographs in order within Aperture, think again. There are lots of tricks and tools that are hidden or not immediately obvious. I have been using the software for years and I'm always finding new ways to do things.

You probably think that you already know everything there is to know about importing images? Then you might be surprised to learn that there are actually lots of options in the import dialog, including many of which people are unaware of. In the following pages you will learn to use these hidden features of the import dialog and you will learn some tricks to speed up your workflow by automating certain tasks during the import stage. You will be shown ways to think about tagging at the import stage and how to make use of tethered shooting. We will also take a good look at Aperture's library structure and some of the ways to make better use of projects and albums. By the end of this chapter, you will be an importing and organizing expert, and hopefully you will save yourself lots of time in future projects. So let's dive right in.

In this chapter you will learn:

- Details and options in the import dialog box
- The difference between managed and referenced originals
- How to add keywords while importing
- How to import directly to an album
- How to create import presets for your camera, and why you should
- How to make Aperture's library work for you
- Understanding Aperture's library structure
- The difference between root-and-project level albums
- How to create project templates
- How to manage multiple libraries
- How to export a project as a library
- Managing RAW + JPEG image pairs
- How to perform tethered shooting

A closer look at the import dialog

When you open Aperture and proceed to import some images, you will get the standard import dialog box. If you've been using Aperture for a while, you've probably seen it hundreds of times by now. If your typical approach is to just import your photos straight to a project then your dialog probably looks a little something like the following screenshot:

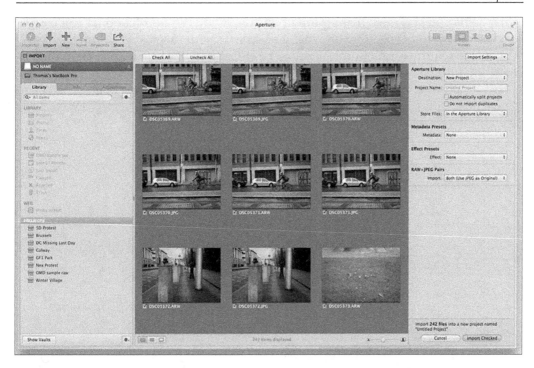

Before we get to the less obvious settings, there is one thing that every photographer should do straight away, and that is to set up the metadata for incoming images. On the right-hand panel of the import dialog box you will see a heading called **Metadata Presets** and a corresponding drop-down menu. If you have already created a metadata preset then you can skip this part. Metadata presets lets you set up a template for inserting metadata into your images. These templates are most useful for information that will be the same in *all* your photographs. So, for example, things such as copyright information, website links, and so on.

If you click on the **Metadata** drop-down menu and choose the **Edit** option, you will see the **Metadata** dialog box. In this window you can create new presets that will contain the set of metadata you insert. This has another useful function too. It controls the fields you see in the import window. To change the fields that are displayed by default in the import dialog box, choose the **Basic Info** preset that should already be visible and take a look at the right-hand column. This column contains a list of metadata fields that you can display. If you want you can enter information in here. The most important thing to know is that, if you check one of the boxes, even if you don't enter any data into the corresponding field in the preset dialog, that will show up in the import dialog box.

What fields you choose to display are up to you. If you are a professional you may need certain fields depending on what you do with your images. Your publisher or editor may require certain information to be embedded in your images. We'll discuss metadata fully in one of the following chapters. But for now, just remember that this is how you turn on and off which fields are displayed in the import dialog box.

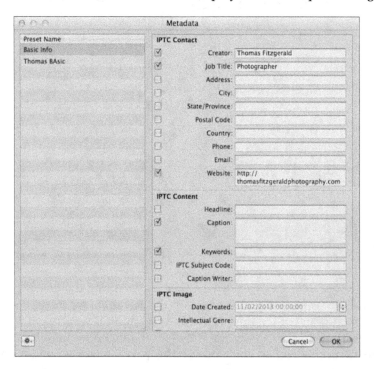

Once you have set your preset and decided which fields you want to be displayed by default, click on the **OK** button to save and exit the presets dialog.

Back in the main import window take a look at the little drop-down menu in the top right-hand corner that says **Import Settings**. This is a menu that allows you to turn on and off options for the import. From here you can toggle the following options:

- **File Info**: This option lets you see information about image files that are displayed in the main portion of the **IMPORT** dialog. If you have turned this option on, clicking on an image will show you information about that image, such as the date it was taken, the image dimensions, its file size, and so on.

- **Rename Files**: This option lets you rename files while importing. It uses the same template mechanism as exporting files does. There are a couple of preset templates that you are probably familiar with from exporting files (I'll cover this in one of the following chapters too). Templates you create for naming files when exporting will show up here as well.

- **Time Zone**: This option lets you offset the time of the captured images to reflect an alternate time zone. You tell it where you were when the camera took the image, where you are now, and it will adjust the time stamp of the imported files accordingly.

- **Metadata Presets**: These options are covered in the earlier section named *A closer look at the import dialog*.

- **Effects Presets**: It used to be called **Adjustment Presets** in a previous version of Aperture. They are the preset recipes for your adjustments of which you may already be familiar with. This option lets you choose a preset to apply to all the images while importing. It's a good idea to set up a default preset for each camera you own and this will be discussed in more detail later in this chapter.

- **File Types**: This option lets you turn on and off which file types are imported. This is extremely useful if you shoot video on your DSLR, for example, but don't want to import the video files into Aperture. Instead of going through the thumbnails of images and manually turning off video files, if you have the **File Types** option enabled, you can just turn them all off in one go. You can also use this option to exclude audio files, exclude audio attachments (some cameras allow you to record an audio note attached to an image), and exclude photos (which is useful if you had previously imported all the photos from a card and now wanted to find the missing video or audio files that you hadn't previously imported). This section also allows you to only include files that are flagged/locked in the camera.

- **RAW + JPEG Pairs**: This option controls how Aperture handles images when you shoot RAW + JPEG in your camera. Personally, I always shoot RAW + JPEG. This section allows you to choose whether to import just the RAW or just the JPEG or both, with either format images as the master. Another really useful option here is **Matching RAW Files**, which allows you to import RAW files that match any JPEG images that you may have previously imported. This can be a very handy workflow if you are on the go and using a low-powered computer or a computer with limited space. What you would do in this situation is import only the JPEG files from your camera. Then you can do your initial culling and edits. Once you have a selection of images you want, you can then import the matching RAW files for just those images. Alternatively, you can transfer the project over to your main workstation and match the RAW files there, keeping all your metadata and editing choices but reapplying them to the RAW versions of your files. I'll show you how to do this in detail, later in this chapter.

- **Actions**: This option lets you apply an AppleScript while importing.

- **Backup Locations**: This option lets you automatically back up files to another location as you import. This is a good idea, especially if you are traveling. I always back up to a mobile drive when importing to my laptop while on the go.

Managed versus Referenced

As you may already know, Aperture lets you store your files in two different ways. When you import images into Aperture, you have the option to either have Aperture manage your files in its library (referred to as **Managed**), or you can have it import your files to a location that you specify on a hard drive (commonly referred to as **Referenced**). When you choose the latter method, Aperture just imports a reference to your image file rather than the whole file. The merits of both approaches are the cause of much debate among Aperture users. Both options have advantages and disadvantages.

On the one hand, if you store your images within the Aperture library, everything is contained in one handy location. A single file is all you need to worry about when it comes to storing, backing up, or moving a library.

 The **library** file is actually a special kind of folder called a **package** that behaves like a single file.

When you export a project in Aperture, it exports it as a library file and that file contain, all the image files within the library if you tell it to. This is exactly the same kind of file as the main library file and you can even switch the current library that Aperture is using to an exported library. You can have both managed and referenced files within your library, and you can choose the method on a project-by-project basis.

If you want to be able to access your files in another piece of software, however, then it makes sense to have your images stored in a folder and imported as references. That way you can go to the folder under the Finder and directly access the RAW or JPEG files from there. Otherwise, to access the RAW files you have to **Export Originals** to another location and you end up with lots of duplicates. Personally, I tend to use referenced when I'm working on my main workstation more often than managed, and I use managed when working on my laptop.

On my workstation all my photos are stored on a large external hardware RAID (Redundant Array of Inexpensive Drives), which is set up using the RAID 5 protocol, which means that the data is protected from a disk failure. When working on my laptop I prefer to have Aperture manage my images, because it means there are less files filling up my laptop's hard drive, and I can keep everything nice and neat in the `Finder`.

Which method you choose is up to you. If it's not something you've ever really thought about then you probably should stick with the managed method. However, if you're more comfortable managing files and folders by yourself, then there are some advantages to using referenced files, especially if you work with other software.

Converting between referenced and managed

Switching between managed and referenced files is actually pretty easy. If you have files in the Aperture library, for example, and you would prefer to have them referenced to a location somewhere on your hard drive, you can carry out the following steps:

1. Select all the images from the **File** menu.
2. Choose **Relocate Originals**.

    Or *control* + click, for a contextual menu.

    This will give you the option to move the original files to a folder on your drive.

To do the opposite, carry out the following steps:

1. Select the images that are referenced.
2. Choose **Consolidate Originals**.

    This will give you the option of moving or copying the image files into the Aperture library, where they will then become managed rather than referenced. If you move the files, they will no longer be in their original location, so you need to be careful with this option if you have other software that is also referencing them.

Adding keywords while importing

One of the options in the **Metadata** section — **Keywords** (if you have enabled it) — is to set what keywords will be applied to the images while importing. This is something that you should think about carefully. First of all, it's a good idea to add some keywords at this stage, but it's also important to realize that the keywords you add here will be added to all the images. You can't add keywords here for specific images. So here are a few tips for thinking about what to add during import. You generally want to be as generic as possible with the keywords you choose at this stage. You can be more specific when you are sorting and organizing.

- If you are just importing images from a specific shoot, use the details of that shoot. So if it's a fashion shoot, for example, some good options might be `Fashion`, `Clothes`, `Clothing`. If you have different models in the shoot, you want to avoid adding the models names or descriptions at this point.

- If you're on a travel shoot, and you're at a particular location such as a city or a country, you could put that in as a keyword, but if you have multiple locations in the images you are importing, choose something more generic such as `Travel`. You could put in the continent as another option, so if you were in Europe, you could put `Europe` down as a keyword.

- Seasons and weather are often good keywords to add. If it was in winter, put down `Winter` as a keyword. You never know when you might need to look for winter images and this will help you find them.

Importing images to an album

Normally, when you import images into Aperture, you import them directly into a project, whether it is a new project or an existing one. However, you can actually import directly to an album too. Here's how to do it in the following:

With the import dialog box open, you will see your library on the left-hand side with all your existing projects and albums. If you want to import into an existing album, simply select the album in this pane. You will notice that the **Destination** on the right changes to the name of the album. If your album is a project album, the images will be imported into the parent project, and will automatically be added to that album.

If you select a root-level album, then the images will be imported to a new project with the date of the first image as its name, as well as being added to the album. This is because all images must belong to a project.

If you don't have an album but want to import to one, you will notice that the **New** button on Aperture's toolbar is still accessible when the import dialog is open, even though other options are grayed out. From here you can create a new album, and again, it can be a project album or a root-level album. I recommend you only use this method for project-level albums, because otherwise you end up with a bunch of oddly named projects.

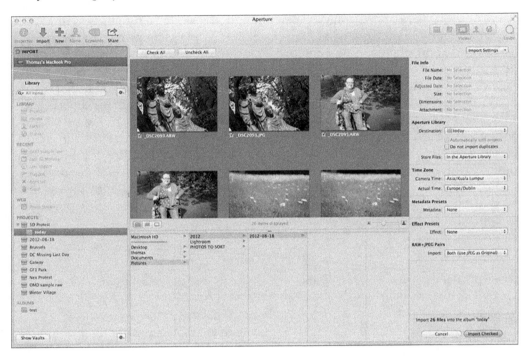

If you're wondering why you would want to do this in the first place, there are plenty of scenarios for why it makes sense. Say, for example, you're doing a travel shoot and you have a project for the city you're in. You might want to break that project down by day or location. Rather than having individual projects, you can store them all in one project and separate them by album, while you could manually sort them into albums after importing this method. This procedure lets you save time and do it during the import session.

Creating presets for your camera

One of the things mentioned earlier is that it is a good idea to create presets for your cameras. You may often find that when you import a RAW file into Aperture it can look quite a bit different from the JPEG or what you saw on the back of the camera when you took the shot. This is because Aperture's interpretation of the RAW file may be different than your camera. Aperture has gotten a lot better at matching the colors of the camera's JPEG images lately though. It used to be that images in RAW could be a lot different from what you expect, but Apple's engineers have become really good at profiling various cameras. Unfortunately though, Aperture doesn't have profiles for individual shooting modes that a camera may support. So, for example, if you have shot using your camera's vivid setting, when you import using RAW, all that nice contrast and vibrancy is lost. If you find yourself making certain adjustments to an image over and over again every time you import, the best thing to do is to create an effect preset. Each camera's RAW files are different, so you should consider creating one for each camera you own and tweak the setting till they are just right. However, you want to be careful when creating effect presets for use during import. They need to be fairly generic and you should avoid using adjustments that need to vary from shot to shot. Here are some do's and don'ts for creating presets to be applied while importing:

Do's	Don'ts
Tweak things such as contrast, black level, definition, and vibrancy	Use a white balance adjustment for an import preset
Adjust Curves tool	Adjust the RAW fine-tuning. These options aren't stored with effect presets.
Tweak the tint, Highlight and Shadows if you need to	
Use a color adjustment to get the colors right for your camera	

Real world examples

Let me give you a couple of examples. First, here is an effect for use on import, which was created for a Fuji X100 camera. The reason that this was created is that, while the RAW files in Aperture are pretty close to the camera's JPEG images, the RAW conversion doesn't support some of the camera's options such as its shadow and highlight tone curves, and also its extended dynamic range. As these options are regularly used when shooting with this camera, a preset was created that mimics these options. This is then selected when importing images from the X100.

The following screenshot shows the settings used in creating this preset:

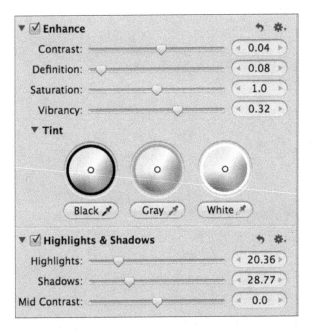

What was done adds a tiny bit of contrast and a little bit of definition because it seemed that the RAW files were a little flat compared to the JPEG files. Some vibrancy was also added to boost the color. To simulate the camera's dynamic range optimization, some Highlight and Shadows adjustments, similar to the ones in the previous screenshot, were added.

For a more complicated example, here is an import effect that was created for the Canon 5D Mark II. In my opinion, Aperture's handling of the RAW files from the Canon is quite a bit off in terms of color. To create a preset, both RAW and JPEG versions of the same images were imported and, using a color adjustment, the settings were manually tweaked until it looked right. It required quite a bit of trial and error and several attempts to get it right. But persistence eventually paid off and the result was a preset that can be applied on import. Some other adjustments were also added, including some slight tint tweaks, very simple curves, and levels adjustment.

You will learn techniques for working with adjustments in a later chapter, but for now, here is a screenshot of the adjustments that were used in this preset:

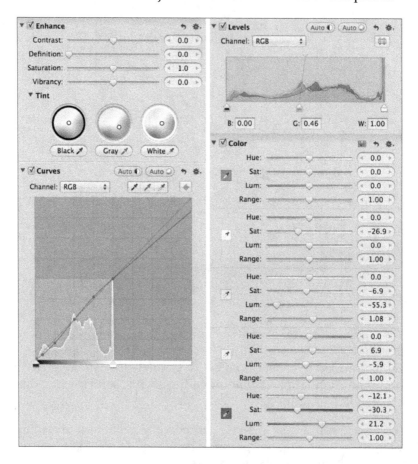

Making Aperture's library work for you

As your Aperture library grows, keeping it organized as you go is the best way to stop it spiraling into chaos. If you're not careful you'll end up with a plethora of unconnected projects and albums and you'll have difficulty finding anything. I know this because I let it happen myself on more than one occasion. Having a good strategy is the key to keeping your library organized, but it's also important to have a good understanding of how Aperture's library is structured. This section is a bit on the technical side, so apologies in advance, but it really is worth knowing, so please bear with it.

Projects, folders, and albums

Aperture's library is organized in a hierarchy, much like a file system on a computer. However, you can also store images in multiple albums, which work like playlists in iTunes. In some ways it's kind of an odd system, as it's neither fully metadata based like iTunes, nor fully file based like the `Finder`. In some respects, it's a hybrid of both. If this all sounds confusing, don't worry, it will become clearer as it is explained further.

Let's start with projects. **Projects** are the most important thing in Aperture. Images *must* be contained in a project (regardless of whether they are referenced or managed). All edits in Aperture are non-destructive because you are never working off the original files. Instead, what you see when you look at an image in Aperture is called a **Version**. Versions are a reference to an original, which is the actual RAW (or JPEG) file. Within a project, you can have multiple versions of an image. Because versions are just references back to the actual file, multiple versions don't mean that the image files are duplicated. They're not, you're just duplicating the reference. Think of it like an alias in the `Finder`. You've undoubtedly used this feature many times if you've been using Aperture for a while, but it's important to understand it from a structural perspective.

Within the Aperture library, you can have multiple projects. You can organize your projects into folders too. **Folders** are the highest level of organization and you can nest folders just like you can in `Finder`. It's important to understand the difference between folders and albums. Folders serve two purposes in Aperture:

- At the root level they can store projects
- At the project level they can store albums

However, you can never have images directly in a folder. Images must be in an album or a project, and always in a project at some stage.

Albums, unlike folders, can contain images. They can be at the root level of the library or at the project level. Albums are essentially playlists. You have undoubtedly made albums before so I won't go into that in too much detail, but it is important to understand the difference between root-level albums and project-level albums.

Root level versus project level

There are essentially two levels of hierarchy in the Aperture library: the root level and the project level. It was mentioned earlier that projects can be exported as libraries, and that's because inside of Aperture projects behave like mini libraries within the main library. There is one big difference though, which is that projects can't contain other projects, so you can't nest projects. When you create an album in Aperture you can create it at either the project level or the root level. You can create an album at the project level for referencing images within the project, although you can add images from other projects to an album. You can also create albums that aren't attached to any projects. These are root-level albums. When you create an album at the root level (that is not attached to any project) you can use it to reference images from any project.

Here's a quick example. Say you have a project full of images, and you select a bunch of them as your selected shots. You then create an album of these named `selects`. You would create this at the project level as it is referencing images within that project. However, if you wanted to keep a running album of all your landscape images, you could create a root-level album named `Landscape` and add images to it from multiple projects.

It used to be the case that if you create a smart album within a project, it will only search for its contents within that project, while a smart album created at the root level will search the entire library. However, in a previous update, Apple added the option to search the entire library within the smart album options. Personally, I never do this as I always create smart albums that reference the whole library at the root level (otherwise it just gets confusing).

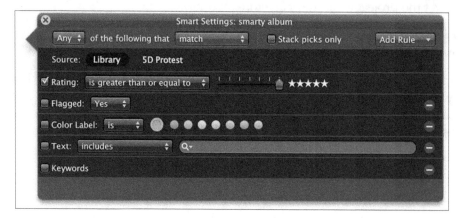

When you create albums at the root level they go in the **ALBUMS** section at the bottom of the library pane of the Aperture window. This is a recent addition too. They used to be lumped in with projects in one big hierarchy whereas now they have their own section. To create an album at the root level, make sure that no projects are selected in the library and then click on the **Add Album** button. You can also drag albums into this section from a project and they become root level. You can organize this section with folders too.

You may be wondering about **Books**, **Light Tables**, **Slide Shows** and **Web Journals**. These all behave exactly like albums, because they're essentially just albums with special properties.

Organizing your library

How you organize your library will depend greatly on the type of photography that you do. There are generally two ways photographers go about managing photos on their memory cards. Some will do a single shoot at a time and some who shoot more casually will gather a lot of different subjects on a memory card from various events before importing the photos. Presented in the following are a few ideas on how you might structure and organize your library. As with many things in Aperture, there are lots of different ways to approach a task, and organizing your library is no different. So the ideas that follow are just a few possible ways you might approach this task. You might have an equally valid approach that you feel more confident about using.

One-shoot-at-a-time approach

If you're working on a single shoot at a time, such as a wedding for example, then organizing your library becomes a lot easier. In this case, you could have folders for each type of shoot and within those folders, your individual projects for each shoot. Let's take the example of a wedding photographer. A typical wedding photographer also might shoot engagement sessions as well as anniversaries. So you would start with root-level folders for Weddings, Engagements, and Anniversaries, and so on for each of the other types of jobs that you do. Inside each of these folders you could have a project for each job, named after the couple. Inside each project you could then break the event down into albums for things such as the arrival at the church, the reception, the rehearsal dinner, and so on. You could then have separate albums or smart albums for your picks and selects.

An alternative method would be to have nested folders for each job. A particular wedding could be the name of the job and this would be a folder within the Weddings folder. Within that folder there are projects for each part of the day and there could also be more albums within the weddings folder to break the project down further.

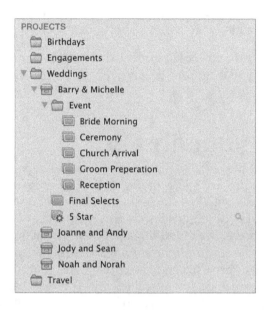

Casual shooting approach

If you are the other kind of more casually organized photographer, one that ends up with a lot of different events in the one memory card, then organizing can be a bit trickier. There are several approaches that can work. You can start by creating folders for each month of the year. Within those folders, import your shoots into individual projects with names for the most common type of shot on the card. So, for example, if you had been doing a photo walk you could name your project photo walk and append the date. You could also create a project called Misc and then when there are images from a session that aren't really appropriate for the project (some shots of your house, for example, which are on your photo walk card), you can copy them to the Misc project.

Outside these set of folders you can create a series of root-level albums for common themes in your photography. These can either be regular albums or smart albums, which you can tie to keywords. If you are doing some long-running photo projects then this can be the way you organize them. Say you are collecting shots of coffee cups, every time you import a shoot to a new project, you can copy any images you may have taken of coffee cups and put them into a coffee cups root-level album.

Using keywords and smart albums

An alternative method that some people prefer to use for sorting photos into albums is to use **keywords**. By adding keywords to your images that correspond to the ongoing projects or the subjects by which you wish to sort, you can use smart albums to curate these. The advantages of this method are that it is generally quicker to apply keywords to images than it is to drag them into an album in the sidebar. The disadvantage is that you have to be careful to use the exact same keyword each time otherwise your smart folder won't pick up the image. You can use the keyword bar to make this easier. I'll show you how to do this in *Chapter 7, Making Metadata Work for you.*

Creating project templates

One of the things that you can do to ease your organizing chores is to create a project template. If you have created a whole set of albums and folders within a project that you find works for you, it can be useful to use this as a template for creating similar projects in the future. This is especially handy if you have created a whole set of smart folders with complex search setups that you really don't want to have to create manually again. Luckily there is a function in Aperture that makes this pretty easy. Here's what to do in the following steps:

1. Select an existing project that you want to duplicate.
2. From the **File** menu choose **Duplicate Project Structure**.
3. Rename the duplicated project.

What this does is duplicate the project, and all included albums, books, folders, smart albums, and so on, only without the images. What you get is a new and empty project with the structure you created, all in place, ready to go.

Merging and splitting projects

You can merge two projects into one if you need to. Simply select the two projects in the library view and from the menu choose **File | Merge Projects**.

The process of splitting a project is a little more involved, but still fairly simple. In the project that you want to split, select the images you want to split into the new project. From the toolbar choose the **New** button and then select **New Project**. This will then pop up a dialog box asking whether you want to move the selected images to the new project. Tick this box, give the project a name and then click on the **OK** button.

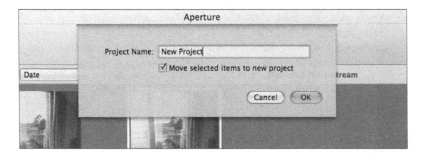

Managing multiple libraries

So far in this chapter we have discussed the structure of Aperture's library in depth, but Aperture can also use and manage multiple libraries. There are many reasons as to why you might want to use multiple libraries. Some people like to start a new library every year. If you are a professional, you might want to keep separate libraries for your work and for your personal photography. If you have several clients for whom you do a lot of shoots, you might want to give those clients their own library. There's also the scenario where you export a project or group of projects as a library and you might need to switch to one of those. With Version 3.4 of Aperture you can now use your iPhoto library in Aperture too.

Switching libraries

Switching libraries in Aperture is a simple technique. To switch between libraries or to create a new library, carry out the following steps:

1. With Aperture running, choose **File | Switch to Library**, and then select the name of the existing library.

2. If you don't see the library that you want to switch to, then choose **File | Switch To Library | Other / New...**.

3. This will open the library chooser window. See the following screenshot:

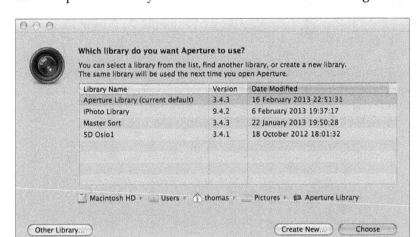

4. If you still don't see the library you want to switch to, then press the **Other Library...** button.

5. To create a new library, choose the **Create New** button.

Exporting a project as a library

To export a project into a new library, start by selecting the project you want to export, and then choose **File | Export | Project** as new library.

To export several projects as a new library, select your projects and from the menu choose **File | Export | Items** as new library.

To export a folder as a new library, select the folder you want to export and from the menu choose **File | Export | Export Folder**.

Note that you can also use the contextual menu to get these options, so select the items you want to export, and right-click or *control* + click on them in the library view and select the relevant menu option.

Importing a library

You can also import the contents of a library into your current library. This will effectively merge the two libraries. To import a library from the menu choose **File | Import | Library**. This will import the entire library including all folders, albums, book layouts, slideshows, and so on into your current library. There are a few things you should know about this process though. If you have images or projects in your current library that are in the library you are importing, Aperture will ask you whether you want to **Add** or **Merge** the libraries.

If you click on the **Add** button, Aperture will duplicate any files in the new library that are in the current one. If you click on the **Merge** button, Aperture will update the metadata and adjustments for the items in the new library that match items in the current library. This is actually extremely useful as it allows you to work on part of your library on another computer and then import the changes back into your main library without having to copy all the image files across. It will simply update the metadata.

Library troubleshooting

If you're having problems with your library, Aperture has some built-in tools to help address any issues that you might be having. Signs of a damaged or corrupt library include things such as thumbnails becoming corrupt, previews not loading properly, or loading for the wrong image, or images not loading at all, and of course, Aperture not loading itself. If you suspect that the library may have issues, you can activate the repair options by holding down *command + option + shift* as you launch Aperture. This will bring up the **Photo Library First Aid** dialog box as shown in the following screenshot:

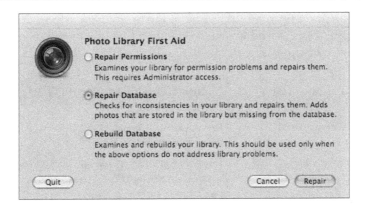

In this dialog box you have three options. The first, **Repair Permissions**, is effective if there are minor issues such as images not loading. However, if you suspect that there is something more seriously wrong with your library, you should try either repairing or rebuilding the database. Choosing **Repair Database** will attempt to correct errors in the existing database file, while choosing **Rebuild Database** will recreate the database from the information contained in the library. But you only need to do this if all else fails.

 Repairing and rebuilding the Aperture database can take quite a bit of time depending on the amount of photos that you have in your library, and the speed of your computer.

Managing RAW + JPEG

If your camera supports shooting both RAW + JPEG simultaneously, and you shoot in this format, there are some considerations to take into account when importing and organizing RAW and JPEG pairs in Aperture. For the most part, Aperture handles this very well. The engineers really seem to have thought the process through when designing this functionality and it can be very useful once you know how it all works.

The first thing to take into consideration is making sure you have the correct settings when importing the RAW + JPEG pairs. As mentioned earlier in this chapter, there are several options that you can select when importing RAW + JPEG. You have the option to import only the RAW files and ignore the JPEG files, or vice versa. You can also choose to have Aperture import both files. When you do this, Aperture keeps them both bundled together, but you are only working off either the RAW file or the JPEG file.

Again, which you are working with is one of the options on import. You can set either RAW or JPEG as the master when choosing to import both. The following table breaks down the options for you:

Both (use JPEG as original)	Imports both files, sets the JPEG file as the file that you are working off of
Both (use RAW as original)	Imports both files, sets the RAW file as the file that you are working off of
Both (separate originals)	Imports both files separately into your library. Be warned that if you do this there is no way to merge them back together
JPEG files only	Only imports the JPEG files. Ignores the RAW files
RAW files only	Only imports the RAW files. Ignores the JPEG files
Matching RAW files	If you had previously only imported the JPEG files, this option will import the corresponding RAW files and link them again

When you have a RAW + JPEG pair in Aperture you can easily switch between them. To do this *control* + click (or right-click) on the image and choose **Set RAW as original** if your image is currently set as JPEG, or **Set JPEG as Original** if your image is currently set as a RAW file.

You can tell which format your image is currently set to by the little badge in the bottom right-hand corner of the image. If it is a little **R** it is set to RAW and if it is a little **J** it is set to JPEG.

If you have an image in one format and you want to create a new version in the other format you have to duplicate it first. So, for example, let's say you have an image that is a JPEG file and you want to have a RAW version to compare it to, but you also want to keep the JPEG version.

To do this carry out the following steps:

1. Select the image.
2. Then *control* + click (or right-click) on the image and choose **new version from original**.

    This will create a new version without any adjustments.

3. Then *control* + click (or right-click) again and choose **Set RAW as Original**.

    If your original is a JPEG just choose the other option.

Note that you can choose to duplicate the version rather than choosing to create a new version from the original. However, you should be aware that any adjustment would be applied to it. This can sometimes be a bad idea as some adjustments work slightly differently when applied to JPEG and RAW files. Also, if you have a preset set on import for your RAW file to better match it to the JPEG as discussed earlier, when you switch to a JPEG, those adjustments will be applied to the JPEG file as well. If you had a contrast adjustment, for example, so that your RAW file matched the contrast of your JPEG, then that contrast adjustment would be applied to the JPEG file, which was already rich in contrast, resulting in an image with too much contrast.

Working with in-camera black and white images

One example of when it might be useful to work with RAW + JPEG is if you are shooting black and white images. Often, when taking black and white photographs, a photographer will use the monochrome picture style in their camera. The problem is, when you import your RAW files back into Aperture, the picture styles are lost. If you shot everything in black and white then it's not really an issue, but if you had mixed black and white and color on the shoot, it becomes a problem when you import the files into Aperture. You will not be able to tell which ones where monochrome and which ones were in color. Luckily there is a fairly straightforward workflow to get around this problem.

It is important to note that for this workflow to work you must set your camera to shoot in RAW + JPEG. Whether you want to use the in-camera black and whites as the final version of your monochrome images, or you want to do your own black and white conversions is up to you. But for this workflow to work, you must start by shooting RAW + JPEG pairs. Once you have finished your shoots, carry out the following steps when working with Aperture:

1. Open the import dialog box and select your source. (Select the card containing your images. Make sure you are importing into a new project.)

2. Under the **RAW + JPEG Pairs** drop-down menu, set your images to import both with JPEG files as originals.

3. Once you have imported all your images go to the browser and make sure you're in grid view by pressing the *V* key to toggle through the view modes until you switch to the grid view.

4. Select all the images that are black and white and label them with a color label. (It doesn't matter which one; just make sure to use a color label and that you use the same one for every image.)

5. If you want to use the in-camera black and white conversion, you can skip this step and go straight to the next one. If you want to use your own black and white effect preset, with the images still selected, apply the effect. Now select all your images by pressing *command + A*. You can now skip ahead to step 8.

6. In the search bar at the top of the Aperture window, click on the magnifying glass icon Q▾ and at the very bottom of the drop-down menu you will see a section for labels. Click on the first circle, which, when you hover over it, the tooltip tells you that it means no label. Choosing this will filter the browser so it only shows images without a label.

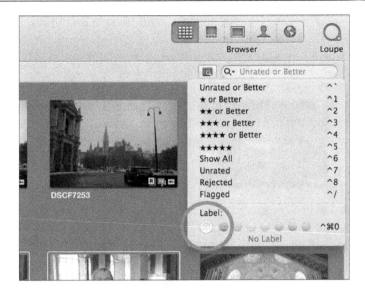

7. If you had correctly labeled all your black and white images, they should now disappear from the window. Now select all your images by pressing *command + A*.

8. From the photos menu choose **Use RAW as original**.

    This should now convert all your color JPEG files to RAW.

9. In the search bar click on the **X** at the right-hand side of the search bar to de-select the filter.

You should now have a project with all your black and white images either set as JPEG files or black and white RAW files, and all your color images set as RAW files. You can also use this technique for other kinds of images too, which don't have to be just black and whites. If your camera supports a particular style that you like shooting with every now and then, but don't use it for every image, then you can use this workflow to isolate those images too.

Shooting tethered

One of the most useful features in Aperture for studio photographers is the ability to shoot tethered. Tethered shooting allows you to connect your camera via its USB cable directly to your computer, and when you begin shooting the resulting photos are immediately loaded into the Aperture library and displayed on your screen. There are a number of advantages to shooting tethered.

First of all, you get a nice big display to view your images on, while on a shoot. This can be invaluable when shooting in the studio as it makes it much easier to evaluate things such as critical focus and the tonality of your images. Secondly, if you have clients present during the shoot it allows them to see the images on a bigger screen rather than the LCD screen on the back of your camera. There's also the added bonus of having the images already captured on your computer, so you don't have to download them off the card later. In addition, you have an extra backup, as most cameras will record to the card at the same time.

Requirements for tethered shooting

Unfortunately not every camera can shoot tethered, and not every camera that can shoot tethered is supported by Aperture. The good news is that most cameras that can shoot tethered are supported. Apple maintains a list of supported cameras on its website. You can find it by going to the following address:

```
http://support.apple.com/kb/HT4176
```

You will also need a USB cable of a decent length, and an open USB port on your computer. I would also suggest going directly into your computer. If you connect to the USB port on an external keyboard, for example (if you're going into a desktop), there may be speed issues, and I've seen cases where hubs can cause problems too. Most people though will more than likely be shooting into a laptop when shooting tethered. The best thing to do is thoroughly test any setup you plan to use before you use it in a mission-critical situation. If possible, the photographer should also have backup equipment available. At least have an extra set of cables to be used if there are connection problems between camera and the computer.

You should also be careful when setting up your camera and laptop. It can be surprisingly easy to pull one or the other and damage them. If you're shooting handheld, you may want to secure your laptop somehow, or at the very least make sure you have a good length on your USB cable. A common setup is some kind of a T-bar mounted on a tripod with a laptop stand on one side and a tripod mount on the other side. These are available commercially from a number of different manufacturers.

Starting a session

To start a tethered shooting session go to the **File** menu and choose **Tether | Start Session**. This will bring up the **Tether Settings** panel:

You may notice that this is quite similar to the options in the import dialog, and that's because they are pretty much the same. At the top, you have the option of **Store Files** for where to store your files. If you don't have a project selected when you start a session, Aperture will create a new one and name it with the date and time when you started the session. The **Store Files** option is the same as when importing normally, and gives you the option to store the files in the Aperture library (managed) or in a location of your own choosing (referenced). You also have the option to rename the files on import and this might be something you want to consider when doing a studio shoot. The **Metadata** section is the same as the import dialog, and again you have the ability to apply presets and set information at this stage. You also have the option to back up files as they're imported and the ability to apply an effect. These options are all the same as the standard import dialog.

A note on RAW + JPEGs

One thing that you might notice is missing though is the option for RAW + JPEG pairs. Unlike a standard import, when shooting tethered, RAW and JPEG pairs are not combined and are treated as separate files. If you have RAW + JPEG enabled on your camera, and start shooting tethered, you will get two images every time you press the shutter button.

A tethered shoot

Once you have your settings set in the **Tether Settings** panel, click on the **Start Session** button to begin your session. This will bring up the tethered shooting HUD. Pressing the **Capture** button on the HUD will cause your camera to take a picture and for it to be immediately imported into Aperture. You can also use the shutter button on your camera.

Note the small checkbox on the bottom left-hand side of the tether HUD that says **Auto Select**. With this checked, every time you take a picture it will automatically become the currently selected picture. So, for example, if you are viewing an image in the viewer, it will be loaded and displayed as soon as you take it. If it's unchecked, only the image you currently have selected will be displayed. If you're shooting and nothing is changing on screen, make sure that this hasn't been accidentally unchecked.

When shooting tethered, your display settings are persistent, so if you zoom in 1:1, for example, it will stay zoomed in when the next image loads. This makes it very handy for checking focus. You can also use the **Loupe** if you would prefer. When shooting tethered, all the other features of Aperture remain active, so you can make adjustments, enter metadata, and so on, all while in a tethered shooting session. This can be very useful if you need to check out potential adjustments and looks on the subject that you are shooting with, while still in the middle of the shoot. This avoids the problem of having models waiting around till afterwards while you test out ideas, in case you need to reshoot something.

Note that you can also close the HUD at any time and continue to shoot tethered, but you will have to use your camera's shutter button. To return to the HUD if you close it, choose **File | Tether | Show Tether HUD**.

Once you have finished your shoot, to end the session simply click on the **Stop Session** button on the HUD and your session will be finished. You can also finish a session by choosing **File | Tether | Stop Session** from the menu.

Summary

In this chapter we took a very detailed look at some advanced options for importing images into Aperture. We looked at both the technique and theory behind some of the things you can do at the import stage to help you better manage your sessions in Aperture. We also took a detailed look at Aperture's library and its structure as well as examining the difference between projects and albums, and how albums at the project level are different from albums at the root level. We also looked at managing the RAW + JPEG pairs, and you learned a workflow for handling black and white images you shoot in your camera. And finally we also covered how to shoot tethered.

You should now have a good understanding of organizing and importing in Aperture. This will lay the foundation for keeping your photos properly organized in Aperture, and it will make your life easier and keep on top of your growing library. In the next few chapters, we will take a detailed look at making adjustments in Aperture. We will cover all the advanced options for processing your images, and you'll learn lots of ways to do some creative and advanced editing right inside Aperture.

2
Advanced Adjustments

Aperture has a surprisingly complex engine for making adjustments. While you might have used it for making basic or even complex tweaks to your images, the technology under the hood lets you do quite a bit more. In this chapter, we will explore some of the more advanced things you can do in Aperture's adjustment panel. To help you become an expert in making advanced adjustments in Aperture, this chapter will give you some in-depth understanding of what goes on under the hood. You will learn the difference between RAW and RGB data, and we will look at how Aperture decodes the RAW image into something that you can use. Once you understand the way Aperture works, you will learn how to approach your editing tasks in a way that works in synergy with the software. Before long, you will be a master at Aperture's adjustment panel and an expert at processing RAW images.

In this chapter we will cover the following subjects:

- Understanding the adjustment tree
- Understanding RAW versus RGB image data
- How Aperture converts an image from RAW to RGB
- Using the RAW Fine Tuning brick
- Setting default adjustment bricks
- Using brushes
- Editing brush masks outside of Aperture
- Cloning and healing
- How to use the Highlights and Shadows tool
- Saving and managing presets
- Advanced sharpening
- Noise reduction in Aperture

Understanding Aperture's adjustment tree

If you want to gain complete mastery over processing images in Aperture, you need to have an understanding of Aperture's adjustment tree. If you know how the software thinks about an image and how it works internally, you will be empowered to make better decisions and work more efficiently within the software. You may be concerned that some of this information is too technical, or that not that important to know, but a little knowledge of the foundation of digital imaging will make you a much better Aperture user. Before we look at Aperture's way of thinking, we first need to look at some RAW basics.

 Much of this chapter deals primarily with RAW images. It assumes that you are working with RAW. If you are shooting JPEG, some of the information here may still be of use, but to get the most out of it you really need to be shooting in RAW.

RAW versus RGB

The first thing that you need to grasp is that, as with any RAW processing software, there are two main processes involved in converting and processing RAW files from your camera. The first involves converting the RAW data to RGB data, and the second involves processing that RGB data. So what is the difference between RAW data and RGB data?

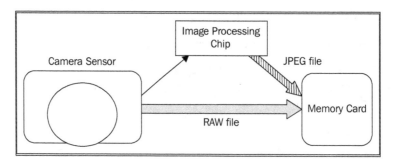

RAW data is the information compiled directly from your camera's sensor, every time you take an image. Normally this data then passes from your camera's sensor to a processor in your camera's body, which then converts this data into a usable format, usually a JPEG. When you shoot RAW, the camera dumps this data to a file instead of processing it on the camera's processor (although it still processes it so you can see a preview).

When you think of image data, you probably think of RGB values and channels containing data for red, green, and blue, or cyan, magenta and more. But RAW files don't store information in such a recognizable way. When light hits a camera's sensor, each of the sensor photo sites record the number of photons hitting the sensor's **pixels**. The photo sites take the electrical charge and convert it to digital information. This information gets stored in a RAW file. It's a bit more complicated than that, but that's the basics of it. In order to be readable by normal software, and in order to be converted into something we can see, the RAW converter needs to convert the sensor data into the standard RGB image data that we are all used to. Because each camera records and processes this information differently, any RAW processing software needs to know how exactly to handle and manage this data, and that's why each camera has its own RAW file format, and that's why, when a new camera is released, you often have to wait for Apple to release an update to support it. Aperture needs to know exactly how to put the data back together in order to make a standard RGB file.

Demosaicing

One crucial part of the conversion process is converting the photon counts on the sensor sites into color data. That might sound fairly straightforward, but the problem is that most cameras don't record light information for each color at each photo site on the sensor. Instead, they use a pattern of red, green, and blue sensitive elements and then an algorithm puts this information back together into a single colored pixel. If you think of how a printer prints in a halftone pattern, which your eyes perceive as a single color, then a camera's sensor is effectively the reverse of this process.

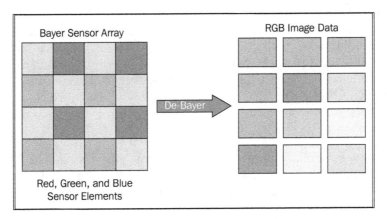

Most cameras use a special pattern for laying out the grid of red, green, and blue photo sites on a camera's sensor, and this pattern is called a **Bayer** pattern after the Kodak engineer who invented it. Most—but not all—cameras use a Bayer pattern.

You may be wondering why all this information is important, but the demosaicing process actually has a crucial impact on your images. The merging of information from several sensor sites to create one pixel, can create aliasing and moiré artifacts. To counter this, most cameras are fitted with an optical antialiasing filter.

This reduces aliasing, but also creates softness. Sharpening algorithms in the demosaicing process counteracts this softness. Aperture allows you to control this process to some extent. We will discuss sharpening later in this chapter, but it's important to understand the difference between sharpening at the RAW level, which is part of the demosaicing process, as compared to sharpening, which is applied to the RGB data.

Linear gamma

Another important thing that takes place during RAW conversion is that a gamma curve is applied to the image data. Because digital camera sensors record image data in a linear fashion, if you were to view them directly, they would be very flat and lacking in contrast.

So what is linear data? Basically, values from bright to dark are recorded in a linear fashion. If you were to graph an increase in brightness between the darkest part of an image and the brightest part as captured by a linear sensor, then the information would be represented as a straight line. The real world doesn't behave like this. Brightness does not scale linearly, and so if you see an image that is purely linear it looks flat and grey.

Because our human eyes do not process data in this linear fashion, and because most analog forms of capture (such as film) record data in a curved fashion rather than a straight line, when you convert a RAW image, cameras apply a contrast curve to the image to make it look realistic. Each camera does its own interpretation of how an image should look and it's this that gives many cameras their own distinctive look. RAW conversion software has to apply this contrast curve too, and when the developers are adding support for a new camera they will create a color profile for the camera. This profile records how that camera interprets the linear data from the sensor and it creates a nice rich image.

You can actually control the amount that this gamma curve is applied, by using the **Boost** slider in the RAW Fine-Tuning adjustment. Turning this off doesn't completely revert the image to a linear gamma, but it gives you some control. This will be covered in the next section.

RGB adjustments

Once the RAW data has been converted to standard RGB image data, all further adjustments take place in RGB space. Aperture, however, has another trick up its sleeve. It does all its RGB processing in 32-bit floating point. What this means is that, unlike most other RAW processing software, Aperture uses 32-bit calculations when processing your image, so adjustments are made using very precise math. This might seem of little advantage, considering most RAW files are either 12-bit or 14-bit at best (some medium format cameras are 16 bit). The advantage, however, comes from being able to perform multiple operations without degrading the image. Also, because floating point math is so precise and of such a high definition, any loss in data integrity is minimal, especially compared to the final 8-bit (per channel) out bit.

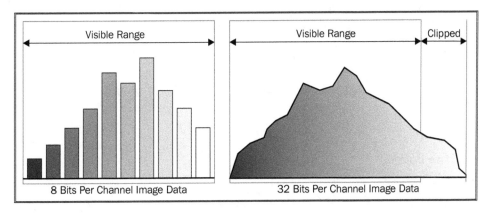

Working internally in 32-bit floating point has another big advantage. 32-bit image data works like HDR (in fact HDR is 32 bit) and can contain values above 100 percent white. This means that if you perform an operation that pushes the values in an image above 100 percent white, that is, the whites are clipped, you can bring those values back into visible range with another adjustment. This makes Aperture extremely powerful. You can add adjustment after adjustment without having to worry too much about image (or data) degradation caused by stacking multiple processes. In my opinion, this is one of Aperture's most powerful features.

Working on RAW data versus RGB data

In Aperture, two adjustments work with RAW data, while the rest work with RGB data. The two that work with RAW data are the **RAW Fine Tuning** adjustment (hidden by default) and the **Exposure** adjustment.

The **RAW Fine Tuning** tab allows you to control some aspects of the RAW conversion process. To access the RAW Fine-Tuning controls for an image, with an image selected, go to the **Adjustments** tab, and from the adjustments tab, choose **RAW Fine Tuning**. This will add a **RAW Fine Tuning** adjustment brick to your adjustment panel. Inside the **RAW Fine Tuning** brick you will see the following options:

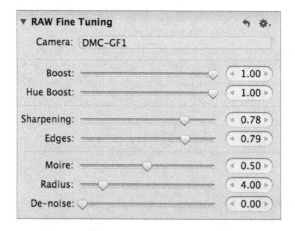

- **Boost**
- **Hue Boost**
- **Sharpening**
- **Edges**
- **Moiré**
- **Radius**
- **De-noise**

Let's go through a few of these options in more detail:

- **Boost**: The first two sliders control the conversion from a linear gamma to a camera-optimized gamma. The first, **Boost**, controls the amount of contrast correction that is applied to an image. This is based on profiling of the individual camera. You normally wouldn't adjust its slider, but there are times when you might want to. Sometimes an image has too much contrast and you might want to bring the contrast values down a bit. This will allow you to do that.

- **Hue Boost**: The second slider, **Hue Boost,** controls how much of the camera's unique saturation profile is applied to an image. This is something that, again, you should rarely need to adjust.

- **Sharpening** and **Edges**: The next two sliders control the sharpening that is applied during the RAW conversion process. This should not be confused with the separate sharpen adjustment that you can apply to an image. Sharpening at the RAW conversion stage is often called **RAW presharpening**. It is used to counter the effects of the demosaicing process and the camera's antialiasing filter. You can adjust the amount of presharpening applied to an image here. Personally I think Aperture's default values are a little high, and I often turn these down, and then add sharpness later using an edge-sharpening adjustment. We'll discuss sharpening in depth a little later in this chapter.

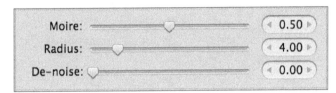

- **Moire, Radius**, and **De-noise**: The next three sliders control noise. The first option is labeled as **Moire** (although the correct term is **Moiré**) and you can use this option to reduce any moiré that may be in your image. There is another use for the **Moire** slider too. If you crank it up, you can use it to reduce the amount of color noise in an image. We will look at noise reduction in depth later in this chapter.

Adding default adjustments

As noted earlier, the RAW Fine-Tuning adjustment is hidden by default, even though it's technically applied to all RAW images. You can change this behavior and have it displayed by default very easily. In fact, if you use any adjustment regularly that isn't part of the default set, you can add it to the default set very easily. Once you do, any adjustment, that you add will appear on every image, even if you don't use them.

To add an adjustment to the default set, simply add the adjustment to an image, and then from the little pop-up menu on the adjustment brick, choose **Add to default set**.

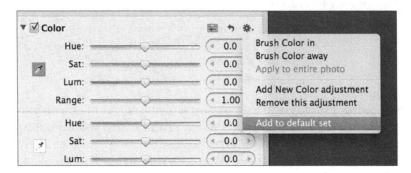

Be aware that this isn't actually adding the adjustment to every image, but merely adding the options to your display, so that you don't have to go to the menu and add that particular adjustment each time.

Personally, I have the following adjustments enabled all the time:

- **RAW Fine Tuning**
- **Chromatic Aberration**
- **Curves**

Multiple adjustments

One of the great features of Aperture is the ability to add multiple copies of an adjustment. This is a very powerful feature, especially when you consider that each of these adjustments can be masked using brushes. There are a few things to be aware of when using multiple adjustments though. If you keep these few guidelines in mind you will make your sessions with Aperture a lot easier.

- Because Aperture is non-destructive, adjustments are not applied one after another, as they would be in Photoshop for example. Instead, the whole adjustment tree is evaluated each time you make a change, and the order can occasionally be important.

- Adjustments are applied from top to bottom. So, in other words, starting with **RAW Fine Tuning** and **Exposure**, each additional adjustment is applied in order as you move down the adjustment panel. This applies too when you have multiple copies of an adjustment. The top one is applied first; then the second one, and so on. Most of the time this doesn't actually make much difference, but occasionally it will. So it's important to be aware of.

- You can't reorder multiple copies of adjustments, and you can't copy and paste or duplicate adjustments. This is an issue when you are creating and using presets. Say, for example, you have two curves adjustments applied to an image, and you want to apply a preset that also has a curves adjustment. This will overwrite the first curves adjustment. There's no way around this and no way to create a new and empty curves adjustment at the top of the stack. (So always apply your presets first!)
- You can only have multiple copies of adjustments that work on RGB data. You can't have multiple copies of either the RAW Fine-Tuning adjustment, or the exposure or white balance adjustments.

The power of multiple adjustments shouldn't be underestimated though, and don't be afraid of using more than one adjustment. Sometimes there is the urge to try and do everything in one go, but if you break it down and split the task over multiple adjustments it can make your job a lot easier. Also, if you are trying to troubleshoot a complex effect, having it broken into smaller steps makes it easier to find out which process might be causing your problem.

For example, if you are trying to fix a burnt-out sky and you find your attempts are darkening the parts of the image, for example, you can always add a second adjustment to correct it and paint it in. Because of Aperture's 32-bit internal processing, you can usually correct undesirable effects of any adjustment with another one, without losing any data integrity, or more importantly, without adding too much noise.

The exception to this is the black area of an image. You can recover highlighted details that get pushed too far, but it's much harder to recover details from the blacks if they become clipped. In this situation, I will add an adjustment to bring the whole value of an image up. Apply another to do whatever operations are necessary, and then use something such as, a curves or levels to bring the blacks back down. Once again, this is possible thanks to the power of Aperture's 32-bit architecture.

Brushes-tips and tricks

Brushes are one of Aperture's most powerful features. Brushes are thought of as being Aperture's way of performing selective adjustments, but a better way to think of them is as a way to mask individual adjustments. As one can have a great number of adjustments, each of these adjustments can be masked so that they only apply to a portion of your image.

You can add a brush mask for almost any adjustment, with the exception of the **RAW Fine Tuning** brick and the **Exposure** brick. See the following steps:

Adding brushes to an adjustment

To add brushes to an adjustment we need to carry out the following steps:

1. From any adjustment brick go to the pop-up menu.

2. If you want to apply brushes to a selective area choose **Brush <Adjustment> in** (where *Adjustment* will be the name of the particular adjustment).

3. If you want to apply an adjustment to most of the image but want a small area without the adjustment applied choose **Brush Adjustments Away**. Or to remove a brush completely, and have the adjustment applied to the entire photo, choose **Apply to entire photo**.

4. When you have a brush applied to an adjustment and you have moved on to working with a different adjustment, you can get back to editing the brush mask by clicking on the little paint brush icon ▱ in the adjustment, as shown in the following screenshot:

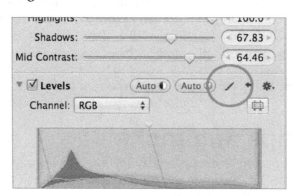

Painting with brushes

Painting with brushes is simple. The brush HUD pops up whenever you are brushing and you have a number of controls, most of which are fairly self-explanatory. The controls are explained in the following:

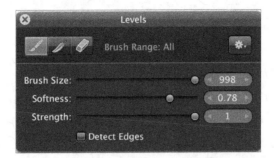

1. **Brush Size**: This option controls the size of the brush. You can set the size from 0 to 1000, although the size is reduced if you have the auto mask turned on.

2. **Softness**: This option controls the amount of feathering on a brush.

3. **Strength**: This option controls the opacity of the brush. (Note that this is not the same as the strength of the adjustment itself. It's only the strength of the brush.)

4. **Detect Edges**: To only have the brush keep to the portion of the image you are painting on, check the **Detect Edges** checkbox. This box tells Aperture to automatically mask the brush based on the area you are over when you start brushing. This resets every time you stop dragging and start a new stroke and is based on the area you are over when you start the stroke.

5. **Eraser**: To erase a brush stroke you can switch to the eraser by clicking on the eraser button. You can also temporarily switch to the eraser by holding down the option key on your keyboard.

6. You can control the way a brush is applied, limiting it to the highlights, midtones or shadow areas of an image. These options are available from the settings cog pop-up menu on the side of the brushes HUD.

7. To remove all brushes from an adjustment and reset the brush mask choose **Clear from entire photo** from the HUD pop-up menu.

There are some things to be aware of when using brushes in Aperture. If you keep some of these things in mind when using Aperture you can save yourself some problems down the road:

1. Brushes can't be copied and pasted. If you need to apply multiple adjustments to the same area you will have to repaint it each time. Try and think whether there might be another way to achieve the same effect with one adjustment rather than several. Alternatively, you might need to consider using an external editor (such as Photoshop) for such an adjustment.

2. There are limits to the softness you can achieve with brushes. If you need to do very fine graduations try setting the strength of the brush low and painting multiple times.

3. Brushes are pressure sensitive, so if you have a Wacom tablet you can control the strength with the tablet's pressure sensitivity.

4. The little crosshair at the center of the brush must be within the image area for a brush to work. If you are trying to paint in a soft edge at the edge of an image, bear this in mind, as there will have to be a portion of the brush at full strength when painting at the edge. Again, painting repeatedly at a low strength can help with this problem.

Editing brush masks outside of Aperture

If you have been using brushes for a while you are probably aware of the limitations of the brushing architecture. It can be very hard to do things such as fine gradients or vignettes with the brush tool. There is a way to get around this problem, but it's not for the faint-hearted. Aperture actually stores brush masks within its library as TIFF files. You can edit these in Photoshop and the results will become the new brush mask in Aperture.

 This section contains advanced techniques and requires some hacking of Aperture's library. Make sure you have a backup copy of your library before attempting to carry out the following steps, and if you are unsure, don't try it.

Editing the brush masks

To edit the brush masks carry out the following steps:

1. Select the adjustment you want to apply the mask to. Brush anything onto the image using a brush. It can be anything like an x or a quick message.

2. **Quit Aperture** (this is very important).

3. Go to your Aperture library in the Finder folder.

4. *Control* + click on the library and choose **Show package contents**.

5. Navigate to the masks folder.

6. Set your Finder view to list view, and view by **date modified**.

7. Find the most recent folder. Its time stamp should be for the time you just created the mask.

8. Open this folder. Inside you should find a TIFF file with a weird name.

9. Open this TIFF file in Photoshop.

10. Do whatever you want to do to the mask in Photoshop. For example, if you want to create a graduated filter, use the gradient tool. Make sure not to change the mode of the image. If you add layers, be sure to flatten the image when you are finished.

11. Save the image. Make sure to choose **Save** and not **Save as**.

12. Quit Photoshop.

13. Re-launch Aperture.

14. You may need to force Aperture to redraw the mask if it is not coming up straight away. To do this, toggle the adjustment on and off.

You can use this technique to do lots of things such as creating gradient filters, or better vignettes, than Aperture's default vignette. You can even use it to create film grain if you are feeling adventurous. Just be really careful you don't touch anything else inside the Aperture library file. You can use this to create presets for things such as neutral density gradients, and your edited brush mask will be stored with the preset.

Cloning and healing

A special type of brush is the **retouch** tool. This allows you to fix things such as dust spots and small areas of an image that you want to remove. Many people just use it for dust spots, but it is actually surprisingly powerful. I have used it personally to remove large sections of an image and the results were seamless.

Using the retouch tool

1. To fix something in an image with the retouch tool (or healing tool), select it from the menu or press X on your keyboard. This will bring up the retouch brush HUD.

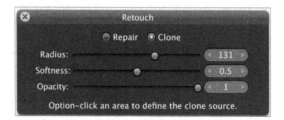

2. There are two main modes of the retouch tool, cloning and healing:

   ° **Cloning**: Cloning requires you to select an area of an image to clone from.

   ° **Healing**: Healing will automatically select an area.

3. For fixing sensor dust spots the healing brush is the best option. Increase the size of the brush so that it's just bigger than the dust spot and click on it. You can actually brush over an area, but for dust spots clicking once will usually suffice. The healing tool works best on skies or other areas of solid color.

4. To clone, select the **clone** tool from the spot removal HUD. This works pretty much the same way as Photoshop. Hold down the *options* key to select an area to clone from and then start brushing.

5. You can delete a stroke by pressing **Delete** in the retouch tool's adjustment brick. You can keep deleting all the way back to the start, but you can't step through the strokes and delete an earlier one. You must go back and delete them one at a time from the latest.

Highlights and Shadows tool

The **Highlights and Shadows** tool is a very useful tool for recovering detail from the shadows and highlights of an image. Apple has actually changed the way the Highlights and Shadows tool works in Version 3.3 of Aperture, and it is now a lot more powerful. One of the big changes Apple made is that it now works with the full floating point extended range data. Previously it only worked in the clipped visible range. This means that you can now recover clipped highlights with it. They also changed the algorithm so that it looks natural.

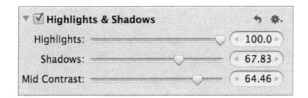

Using the Highlights and Shadows tool

To use the Highlights and Shadows tool carry out the following steps:

1. To apply the Highlights and Shadows adjustment, check the **Highlights and Shadows** checkbox from the **Add Adjustment** menu at the top of the adjustment panel.

2. To bring down blown highlights or reduce the intensity of the highlighted areas of your image, drag the highlight slider to the right.

3. To bring out detail in the shadows, drag the **Shadows** slider to the right.

4. If you drag these sliders too far, you may reduce the contrast of the image and find that it looks a little flat. Luckily, the Highlights and Shadows tool includes a third slider designed to compensate for this. Drag the **Mid Contrast** slider to the right to increase the contrast of the midtones and fix the flatness that can be introduced when using the Highlights and Shadows tool.

The Highlights and Shadows tool may look deceptively simple, but there are some tricks that you can use to get more out of it.

1. You can use the **Mid Contrast** slider on its own. This will add contrast to the midtones without affecting the blacks and whites of the image. This is different from the contrast in the **Enhance** brick, which does affect the blacks and whites.

2. If a previous adjustment pushes the whites of an image outside the visible range and your image is clipped, you can use the Highlights and Shadows tool to bring the clipped image data back into visible range.

3. Dragging the sliders will give you values of between 0 and 100. However, you can manually enter numbers above 100 into the fields.

4. You can have multiple Highlights and Shadows adjustments. If you are trying to recover particularly difficult shadows, it may be more advantageous to add multiple shadow and highlight adjustments and set the values a bit lower with a touch of mid-contrast rather than trying to do it all in one go with one adjustment. You can also use the brushes functionality to mask a Highlights and Shadows adjustment to a particular area.

Saving, editing, and managing effect presets

Effects are an invaluable part of Aperture. They allow you to save recipes of adjustments for reuse. You can even share them with other computers or even other Aperture users. Saving and editing presets might not seem like that advanced a feature, and anyone who has been using Aperture for a while has undoubtedly worked with effects by now, however, there are a lot of little tips and tricks to consider when working with effects.

Saving an adjustment recipe as an effect preset

To save an adjustment recipe as an effect preset carry out the following steps:

1. To save an effect, select an image that has some adjustments applied to it, and from the effects menu choose **Save Effect**.

2. This will bring up the **Effect Presets** window (refer to the following screenshot). Here you can name your effects.

3. On the right-hand side of the panel you will see a list of adjustments that are going to be saved with your effect. These are the adjustments currently applied to the image. If you don't want to include all these adjustments you can simply click on the delete icon 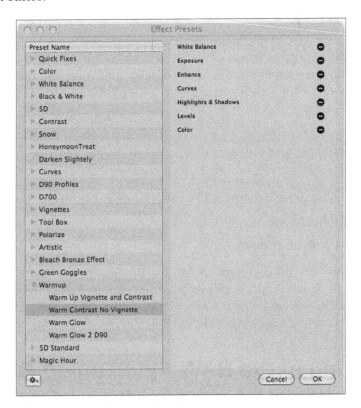 beside the ones you want to lose.

4. You can also create folders to keep your effects in. This allows you to group them according to your needs. For example, if you have a set of presets for creating nice black and white images, you can save these in a `Black and White` folder.

5. When you are finished you can then click on **Save** to save and exit out of the effect editor.

The non-destructive nature of editing images in Aperture means that, when you make adjustments, you are never actually editing the original image. Instead, Aperture stores a set of instructions as to what to do to an image, and these are applied every time you view or export that image. Because this set of instructions is independent of the actual picture data, you can reapply this set of instructions to a different image. This is essentially what you are doing when you create an effect. You are saving this set of instructions as a recipe that you can then apply to other images.

You can go back and edit existing presets at any time. However, you are limited as to what you can do. You can delete adjustments from an effect, you can rename it, and you can put it in a folder. You can also reorganize the existing folders, and export and import effects from these folders.

- To bring up the effects editing panel, choose **Edit Effects** from the effects pop-up menu at the top of the adjustments panel.

- To export an effect, select the effect, or a folder of effects, and choose **Export** from the cog pop-up menu at the bottom.

Sharpening

Sharpening your images is essential in digital photography because of the way the demosaicing process softens images. It is often perceived to be a tricky technique to master because the controls involved can appear confusing and difficult to figure out. With a little knowledge though, you should be able to get the most from sharpening in Aperture.

There are three places in Aperture where you can sharpen your images. These all work a little differently, and will give you different results. The three are mentioned in the following:

- RAW presharpening, in the **RAW Fine Tuning** controls
- Sharpen adjustment
- Edge sharpen adjustment

Of the three, Apple doesn't recommend you use the **Sharpen** adjustment. According to the Aperture documentation, **Sharpen** has been superseded by **Edge Sharpen** and is only provided for backwards compatibility. **Edge Sharpen** is a much more powerful and accurate sharpening tool, and it is wise to use this instead of **Sharpen**.

Sharpening in the RAW Fine Tuning Brick

First let's talk about RAW presharpening. In the **RAW Fine Tuning** brick, Aperture has two sharpening controls: **Sharpening** and **Edges**. These apply sharpening during the demosaicing process and are used to compensate for the softening effects of a camera's antialiasing filter and the DeBayer algorithm. **Sharpening** controls the amount of sharpening, and **Edges** basically controls the radius. These controls are pre-configured at various settings depending on the camera.

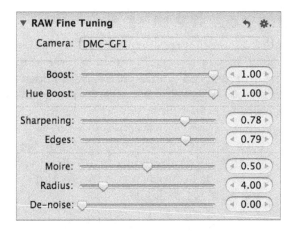

The RAW fine-tuning sharpen settings should not be used to add sharpness to your image. You should only use it as an initial sharpening pass to compensate for the inherent softness of the RAW process. Resist the urge to crank it up full. It's a blunt force instrument and the results can be quite crude. If anything, in my own personal opinion, the default settings are often too high and I regularly turn it down and use edge sharpening instead. It's also important to note that too big an amount of initial sharpening might increase visible noise if used on images taken with a high ISO value.

Edge sharpening

If sharpening in the **RAW Fine Tuning** section is a blunt instrument, then edge sharpening is a fine surgeon's scalpel. **Edge Sharpen** applies sharpening in three passes and you can control the amount that is applied, the threshold of which is considered an edge, and the blending between the passes. This may sound a bit intimidating at first, and the settings the tool keeps in default will look bad initially, and this can put people off using it, but once you know how, the results can be pretty good. The important thing to note about edge sharpening is that there is a process of using it, and that the default settings are designed with the beginning of this process in mind, rather than an end result. The other thing to understand is that, as with all sharpening, **Edge Sharpen** isn't really sharpening at all. It's creating the illusion of sharpening by adding contrast between edges.

Understanding how it works

To get your head around what is happening, here's an analogy using traditional image editing terminology. If you were in Photoshop, for example, and you ran a **Find Edges** filter on your image, you would get a series of lines and curves where the edges of your image are. This would be the parts of your image that **Edge Sharpen** adds contrast to. The **Edges** slider would be the threshold as to what is considered an edge. In other words, how much contrast there needs to be between areas of an image before it's considered to be an edge. If you were then to use this edge tracing as a mask to apply a contrast adjustment, then the **Intensity** would be the amount, and **Falloff** would be how much you would blur the mask. This isn't exactly how it works, but it's a close analogy.

To apply edge sharpening correctly, and because the settings that will work will vary from image to image, you need to follow a workflow when using edge sharpening. Note that to see the results of sharpening properly you will need to zoom into your image so you're viewing it at 1:1.

Here's what to do when you want to use edge sharpening:

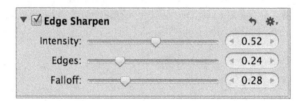

1. Add **Edge Sharpen** from the **Add Adjustment** pop-up menu.

2. Bring the **Intensity** up to the maximum value. This will allow you to see the edges more clearly, so you can determine what is being considered an edge.

3. Adjust the **Edges** slider till you get what you want to be considered an edge in the range of the sharpening control. Basically you want to make sure it's not affecting large flat areas of color and ramping up any noise.

4. Adjust the **Falloff** until it looks more natural and the edges aren't too obvious. One thing to note about falloff is that it behaves the opposite of what you would expect. Lowering the value actually makes the transition smoother and has less parts of the image sharpened.

5. Reduce the **Intensity** slider back down so the whole effect is subtle and natural-looking.

Selective sharpening

Because you can brush in (or out) the edge sharpen adjustment just like you can with any other adjustment, you can use a brushed edge sharpen adjustment to selectively sharpen an area of an image. Just apply a brush to the adjustment. Alternatively, if you want to have sharpening all over, but want one area extra sharp (such as a model's eyes) you can add a second edge sharpen brick and brush that in.

Be careful not to oversharpen

When sharpening your images you always want to be careful not to oversharpen them. One of the quickest ways to kill an otherwise good image is to oversharpen it. Over-sharpening gives an image a false, digital look and can really ruin a good picture. It's surprisingly common too, especially among novices. If you look at many of the popular photo-sharing sites you'll find image after image that has been processed and sharpened to the point of looking ridiculous. When sharpening, remember not to go too far. Your image should have crisp edges, but not rings or halos around them, and areas of flat color shouldn't be full of patterns and noise because you oversharpened the image. It's also important to be aware that many online services such as Flickr and Facebook add additional sharpening when they scale images for display, so this can further exaggerate any oversharpening.

Noise reduction

Noise is a constant problem in digital imaging, although modern cameras are getting better and better at handling noises in the images they capture. Noise in digital photography comes from two main sources.

The first is high **ISO noise**. This occurs when you turn up a camera's ISO and the increased sensitivity results in a noisy image. Cameras are getting better and better at this and it is becoming less of an issue, however, it is still a problem at extreme sensitivities.

The other area where noise occurs is when you push the exposure of an image and you recover details from the shadow areas. Some cameras are better than others, but because of the way digital imaging works, there is less data in the lower half of an image's brightness values than the top half (this is why people often suggest shooting **to the right** to optimize the quality of digital images) and when you recover details from the shadows you can often encounter noise. The level of noise varies from camera to camera, and some are better than others.

There are two adjustments you can use to reduce noise in Aperture. The first is in the **RAW Fine Tuning** brick. The second is a **standalone noise reduction adjustment**. The standalone adjustment is a legacy adjustment, and it is not as good as the more recent RAW fine-tuning options. The only reason you should ever use the standalone adjustment is if you have shot a JPEG image and you need to reduce the noise in it. It's not very good though, so unless you really need to use it, you would be better off using a third-party solution which will be covered in a later chapter. For the rest of this chapter we will discuss the options in the RAW fine-tuning section.

Chroma versus luminance noise

There are two types of noise that typically occur in digital images. Chroma, or color noise, and luminance noise. **Chroma** noise manifests itself as blotches of color on your image. It is the most digital-looking of noise and it is quite unpleasant to look at. **Luminance** noise is more like traditional film grain and, depending on the camera, it can actually be *okay* to look at it, in that it can add a nice grain to the image. There are limits, of course, and too much luminance noise is just as much of a problem. But you can generally live with more luminance noise than chroma noise.

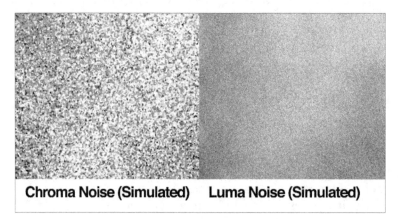

Chroma Noise (Simulated)   Luma Noise (Simulated)

Noise reduction options in RAW fine tuning

There are three sliders that control noise reduction in the **RAW Fine Tuning** section of Aperture. These are:

- **Moire**
- **Radius**
- **De-noise**

You may be wondering what the first two have to do with noise reduction. The **Moire** slider is normally used for controlling the color artifacts caused by repetitive patterns hitting the linear grid of photo sites on your camera's digital sensor. If your camera has no antialiasing filter, you may often encounter moiré. Even with an antialiasing filter, many cameras still suffer from aliasing problems.

The **Moire** slider has another little trick up its sleeve though. It can reduce the amount of chroma noise in an image. It's not perfect, and not as good as some of the dedicated color noise reduction offered in some other software, but it does work. You use this in combination with the **Radius** slider to control the strength of the effect. Generally, if you need to reduce chroma noise in an image, crank the values up full.

The third slider, **De-noise**, is used to control luminance noise. You simply drag the slider to the right to control the amount of noise reduction. You should be careful though, because the **De-noise** option will soften your image substantially, and after about 0.5 on the slider, it starts to look ridiculous. I recommend keeping the values between 0.25 and 0.5 at the most (the lower the better).

Getting the best noise reduction results in Aperture

Aperture has something of a bad reputation when it comes to noise reduction. It has lagged behind some of its competitors when it comes to adding modern noise reduction algorithms. However, with a little careful thinking and a somewhat unorthodox workflow, I believe you can still get pretty good results. Here's my five-step technique for getting good noise reduction results in Aperture.

 This only works with RAW files.

1. Turn RAW Sharpening off: RAW sharpening is applied before noise reduction, so it's basically amplifying noise before you then go to reduce it.

   You will get much better results if you turn sharpening off completely in the RAW fine-tuning section before doing any noise reduction.

2. **Set Moiré and Radius to Maximum**: This will reduce any color noise that might be in the image.

3. Set the **De-noise** slider to somewhere between **0.2** and **0.5**: Don't go higher than 0.5 as it will oversoften the image.

4. Add an edge-sharpening adjustment: Set the **Intensity** to 0.5, the **Edges** to 1, and the **Falloff** to 0.5.

5. Drag the **Edges** slider in the **Edge Sharpen** adjustment down slowly till it looks the best.

This should give you a reasonable level of noise reduction without making your image too soft. You may have to adjust the sliders a bit to best suit your own image, but this should get you in the right ball park.

Summary

In this chapter, we took a detailed look at making advanced adjustments in Aperture. We started by looking at the fundamentals of how a RAW file works, what it is, and how it's decoded in Aperture. We looked at the differences between RAW data and RGB data. We covered how to set up your adjustment panel to include your most commonly used adjustments by default. We looked at some advanced topics, such as how to use brushes, and how to edit brushes outside of Aperture. We also covered the important subject of sharpening and noise reduction, and you learned some valuable tips on using different kinds of sharpening.

Hopefully, after reading this chapter, you will have the knowledge to be able to tackle most tasks in Aperture. You've been given a good grounding in the theory behind the adjustments, so you will be better able to make your own decisions. Of course, one of the great features of Aperture is that there are many different ways to accomplish the same task. You should now have a better understanding of the way the advanced features work and you can experiment and find your own techniques.

One thing that you may have noticed, however, is that we didn't cover the Curves adjustment in this chapter. That's because curves is such a powerful feature that the **Curves** tool gets a whole chapter all to itself, and we will go into that in great depth in the very next chapter. After that, in *Chapter 4, Aperture in Action*, we will take a look at some examples of real world tasks that you may come across in your photography.

3

Everything You Ever Wanted to Know about Curves

The Curves adjustment is one of the most powerful tools in Aperture. With the Curves adjustment and a little bit of knowledge you can achieve just about any kind of effect you might want.

The Curves tool is one of the oldest tools in the digital imaging toolset. It's been there since the earliest versions of Photoshop, and pretty much every other major digital image manipulation software features Curves in one form or another. The funny thing is, Aperture didn't have a Curves adjustment until Version 3. When Aperture was first released, long-time digital imaging professionals screamed out decrying the lack of a Curves tool. Aperture's designers thought that the enhanced levels tool would suffice, but still users demanded Curves functionality. The cries were finally heard in Version 3. Apple didn't just give Aperture users a standard Curves tool. However, they went one step further and gave Aperture users a Curves tool on steroids.

Amazingly enough, despite its heritage, Curves is a surprisingly under-used tool. A lot of people don't quite u

nderstand how it works, or find it daunting, and so never properly learn how to use it. It really is worth taking the time to understand it though, and if you're one of those people who never fully explored Curves, hopefully once you've read this chapter you'll appreciate the power of this seemingly simple tool.

In this chapter you will learn:

- The basics of how Curves work
- How to understand a histogram
- How to change brightness and contrast with a Curves adjustment
- How to work with extended range data in Aperture's Curves tool
- How to warm up or cool down an image with a Curves adjustment

- How to tint Shadows and Highlights with a Curves adjustment
- How to darken skies with a Curves adjustment
- How to create a vignette with the Curves tool
- How to create a highlight roll-off using the Curves adjustment

Curves basics

This section is for those who have never used a Curves adjustment before. It will give you a grounding in the theory behind tonal curves and also how to use them. If you are already familiar with the basics of the Curves adjustment or have used tonal curve controls in other software before, feel free to skip past to the next section.

To understand how the Curves adjustment works, you must first understand how a **histogram** works. To do that, you must learn how to look at your image in terms of its tonality or brightness level. If you break down your image into the shadow areas, the midtones, and the highlights, you'll begin to see how the software sees your image. Now imagine that there are tones in between these tones. In fact, consider that every value of brightness from the darkest to the lightest parts of your image gets measured. If you were to plot the number of pixels in your image at each brightness level on a graph, you get something that looks like the following diagram:

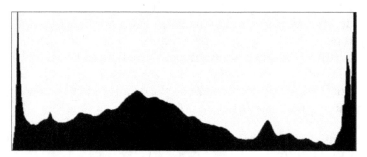

If this looks familiar it is because we have just described how a histogram works. You'll see the histogram at the top of the adjustment tree in Aperture, and if you have a Curves adjustment applied, you'll see a histogram there too. So a histogram is a graph of all the pixels in your image at each brightness level.

If that's a histogram, then what are Curves? If you consider your unedited image to be the starting point, then consider that any adjustment that you might make would be a deviation from this straight line. Because we haven't actually made any adjustments yet, the line is straight at the start, and this is the baseline. In essence what a Curves adjustment does is that it allows you to control the response of the brightness levels within your image for any given brightness value.

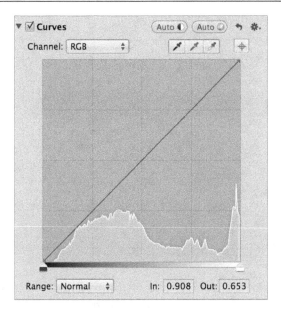

That may sound a bit like technical jargon, so in plain English it means that, for every shade of brightness within your image, with Curves you can tell that area to be brighter or darker. So, for example, you can tell the shadows to be brighter, or the midtones to be darker. If you're thinking that it doesn't sound very powerful at all, then you need to also understand that you can do this kind of manipulation on each of the individual red, green, and blue channels that make up an image. Effectively you can control the colors in an image as well as brightness with Curves. Not only that, but you can also control the color within the different brightness zones of an image too. For example, you can make the midtones warm while also making the shadow areas cooler.

When you combine the typical Curves tool that you get in many software packages with some of the unique features in Aperture, you get an even more powerful tool. You can brush any Curves adjustment in (or out), and you can have multiple Curves adjustments. You can also use the Aperture Curves adjustment to manipulate values above 100 percent brightness, with the extended range functionality, and bring those values back into the visible spectrum.

Referring to the tones in an image

There are standard terms used to describe the tonality of your image. You may already know these, but if you don't, here is a quick primer in the following of this section:

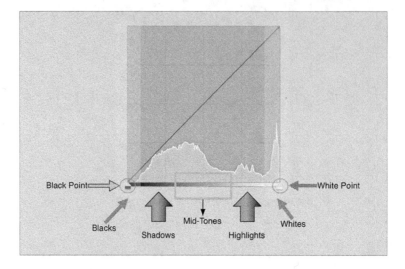

- **Black Point**: This is the darkest part of the visible range of any image. It is what is considered to be zero brightness. If you used an eyedropper on it, the RGB values would be at 0. If you have a low-contrast image, the darkest pixels in your image may be well above the black point. You can adjust the black point with a number of tools in Aperture, including the Curves tool. (And the dedicated black point slider.)

- **Blacks**: Not to be confused with the black point, the blacks in your image are generally the darkest parts of an image, and the very lowest part of the histogram.

- **Shadows**: The shadow tones in an image are generally considered to be the tones in an image that would be graphed on the lower quarter of the histogram. You can see the area that is considered to be **Shadows** on the previous diagram.

- **Midtones**: As the name implies, midtones occupy the center of the histogram, and are general areas of midbrightness.

- **Highlights**: Highlights are the opposite of shadows, and are generally considered to occupy the upper quarter of the histogram.

- **Whites**: At the very top of the histogram are the whites. These are the brightest parts of your image.

- **White Point**: This is the absolute brightest point in your image. The white point is the top of what is considered visible range. You can adjust the white point just as you can adjust the black point. With Aperture's extended range curves, you can adjust the white point upwards to bring more image information into the visible range.

Putting the Curves in the Curves adjustment

Before you start to learn how to do certain things with Curves, you need to first learn how to manipulate the curve itself. As you'll quickly see, there's a reason it's called Curves.

To start, you need to add a Curves adjustment to any image. You can do this by choosing **Curves** from the **Adjustments** pop-up. Now, move your mouse cursor over to the diagonal line (the Curves line) in the **Curves** window till it changes to a crosshair.

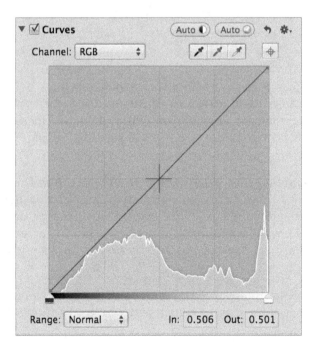

Now click your mouse and this will create a point on the curve. Drag this point up or down vertically. Notice how the line is now a smooth curve between the three points in the following screenshot:

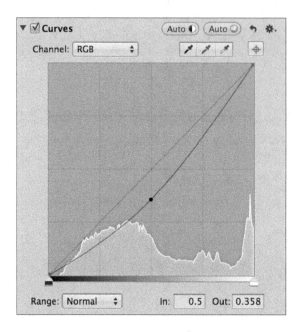

The line will always try to draw a smooth curve between three points. Remember this, because it will make your life a lot easier when you're going to do complex curve manipulations. Say, for example, you want to increase the curve on the lower part of the histogram but you want to keep the top part flat. Let's try it and see what happens.

Add a point in the middle. Now add another point between the middle and the left-hand side of the graph. As soon as you start dragging this point (that you just added) down you'll notice that the top part of the graph is now curving up. This is because the Curves tool will always try to create a smooth curve. To get around this, think of this as the three-point rule. Always add three points if you want to control the curve over the whole graph.

Let's try our example again. Reset your curve by clicking on the reset arrow in the top right-hand corner of the Curves adjustment window as shown in the following screenshot:

Add the center point to the curve again. This time add two points to the right of the curve, on the brighter side. Keep one fairly near the center point, and one in the middle between the center-most point and the right-hand point.

Now add the point on the lower side, as we did before, and drag it down. Notice how the top part stays fairly straight this time.

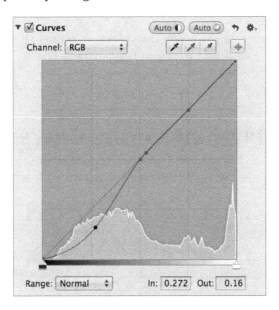

If you move the point significantly you will still create a curve on the top, but you can just add another point to correct this. Most of the time though, three points are all you need.

If you want to get rid of a point on a curve, drag it to the far left or right of the curve and it will disappear. Sometimes this can be a bit tricky and you have to wiggle it a bit to get it to disappear. If you have selected a point on a curve, it can also be removed by pressing the *Delete* key on the keyboard.

Now that you know how to manipulate the curve, let's move on to actually doing something useful with it.

Controlling contrast and brightness with Curves

Controlling brightness and contrast is the most basic thing that you can do with Curves. You're probably thinking why would you want to do this when you have a perfectly good brightness and a contrast slider in the exposure adjustment?

There are a couple of reasons. First of all, the sliders in the exposure brick behave differently than the Curves tool. Also, you may want to brush a brightness adjustment in at some point and you can't brush the exposure adjustment in, so it's useful to know how to do it with Curves. Let's start with brightness as it's the easiest.

Controlling brightness with Curves

Start by adding a Curves adjustment from the **Add Adjustment** pop-up menu. Add a point in the center of the curve and then carry out the following steps:

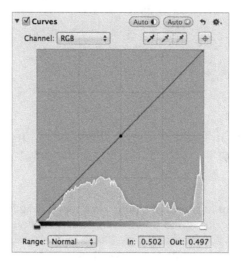

1. To increase the brightness in the image drag the point up, as shown in the following screenshot:

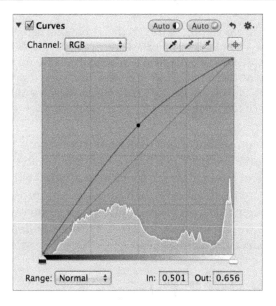

2. To decrease the brightness drag the point down, as shown in the following screenshot:

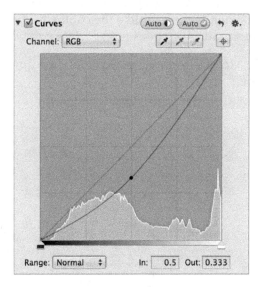

You may be wondering what exactly is going on here? As we discussed earlier, the straight line is the baseline of the brightness values in your image before you edit it. When you drag the curve up you're increasing the values away from the baseline, and when you drag down you're decreasing the values. Because it's a curve, there's a nice smooth transition to the values.

One of the things that you will notice is that when you make a brightness adjustment using Curves, you're not affecting the whites or the blacks, so you don't cause any clipping. Compare this to adjusting the exposure of an image that does cause the whites to clip if you increase the exposure. If you use Aperture's brightness slider in the exposure adjustment brick, it performs the exact same way as a curve, and this is essentially what we are doing here. The brightness slider can't be brushed in however, whereas a Curves adjustment can.

Contrast and the S-Curve

Adding contrast with the Curves tool is just as easy as adjusting brightness. Unlike brightness though, using Curves for contrast gives a different result than using Aperture's Contrast adjustment. Using a Curves adjustment can be a better option than using the contrast slider, because unlike the contrast slider, the Curves tool doesn't clip the brightness values of your images when you use it to add contrast.

1. To add contrast, start by adding a point at the first quarter of the graph (on the first grid line).

2. Add a second point on the last quarter or the third grid line.

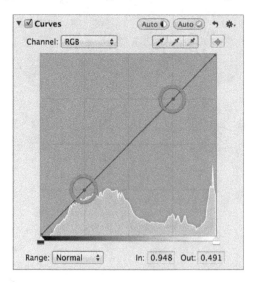

3. Now, drag the first point down just a little and the second point up till you have something that looks like the following screenshot:

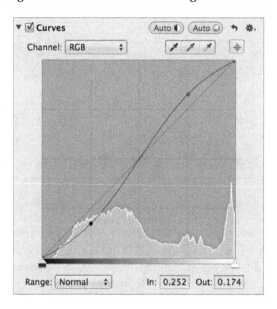

Notice that your image now has more contrast. The amount you move the points, controls the amount of contrast you add.

 This type of curve is often referred to as an S-curve, because it's in the shape of the letter S.

The difference between contrast with Curves and the contrast slider

You may be wondering what the difference is between the contrast slider and adding contrast with a Curves adjustment. To illustrate this, load up an image in Aperture and take a look at the histogram as you drag the contrast slider up and down. Notice how it expands out from left to right. It's as if you took an image of the histogram and scaled it horizontally.

You'll notice too that values will clip quickly and whites will get pushed beyond visible range, and the blacks will be clipped at the bottom of the graph.

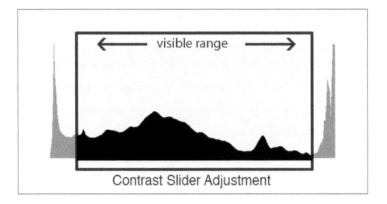
Contrast Slider Adjustment

With Curves, you're never changing the black point and white point values, so they never get clipped or crushed. Think of it as if the histogram is a sheet of rubber, and both ends are stapled down. What you're doing then is pushing the left and right sides towards the end without actually affecting the ends.

Creating a high-key and low-key look

You can expand upon the standard S-curve to create a basic high-key and a low-key look. Start with the basic S-curve from the previous example in the *Contrast and the S-Curve* section.

A **high-key** look is traditionally created through lighting and exposure at the time of taking a photograph. It is the act of deliberately overexposing an image to create a bright, washed-out look. While it is often done in-camera, you can create a faux high-key look for your images in post-production.

A **low-key** image look is one in which the photographer has deliberately underexposed the image so that it contains mostly dark tones.

To create a high-key look, drag the right-hand point (the brighter side of the curve) higher till you end up with something like what is shown in the following screenshot:

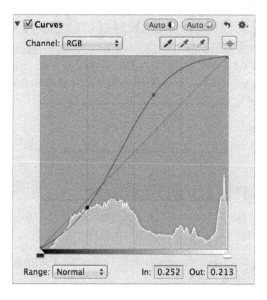

This will give a nice high-key type effect to your image without clipping the whites.

To create a low-key look, do the opposite and drag the lower point down further as shown in the following screenshot:

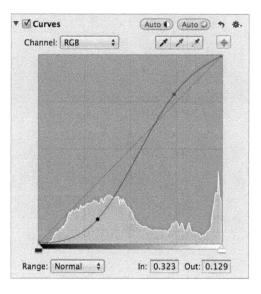

You can then add additional points to give you greater control over the curve if you need to.

Warming up and cooling down

Now that we have learned how to use Curves to adjust brightness and contrast, let's have a look at how to use Curves to adjust colors in an image. The principle is basically the same, except you are adjusting the individual channels instead of the overall brightness.

To select a channel, choose the channel from the channel pop-up at the top of the Curves adjustment and select the channel you want to adjust.

Adding warmth to an image

To warm up an image follow these simple steps. You can control the amount of warmth by the distance you move the points on the curve.

1. Start by adding a Curves adjustment. From the **Channel** pop-up menu, and then choose the **Red** channel.

2. Create a point in the middle of the graph for the red channel. Drag this up a little. Don't go too far or the effect will be overpowering.

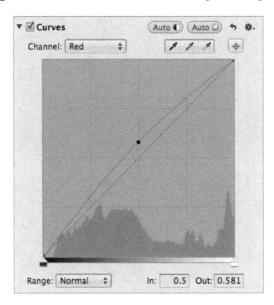

3. Now switch to the **Blue** channel, add a point in the center of the curve, and drag this point down as shown in the following:

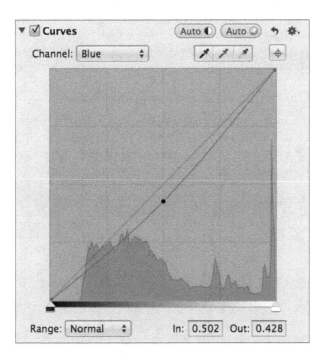

Your image should now be nicely warmed up. The amount you drag the red middle-point up will control the amount of red you added to the image, but you need to balance it by reducing the blue channel or it will become red rather than warm. It will take a bit of playing around to get the values right to where you want them.

Cooling down an image

If your image is too warm and you want to cool it down, you need to do the reverse of what was in the previous step. In this case, you would drag the point on the blue curve up and the point on the red curve down.

Tinting shadows and highlights with Curves

The beauty of Curves is that it's not limited to affecting all areas of the image. For example, if you wanted to just add warmth to the shadow for example, you can easily do that using Curves. The same goes for tinting the highlights.

Tinting shadows

Let's start by looking at how to tint shadows. In the start of this chapter, we looked at how to limit our editing to the bottom part of the curve. We will use the same technique to tint the shadows. As an example, we will warm up the shadows, but you can use the same method to add cooler tones, or even green or some other color to the shadow portion of an image.

1. Start by adding a Curves adjustment to your image.

2. Switch to the **Red** channel on the Curves adjustment controls. Add a point in the center of the curve. Add another point on the graph just to the right of this and add a third point at the intersection of the third graph line. It should look something like the following screenshot:

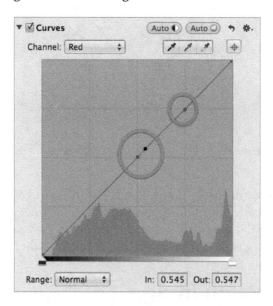

3. Now add a point at the intersection of the first graph line and drag it up a little. You will notice that your shadows now have some red in them. Adjust the curve point till you get the level where you want it.

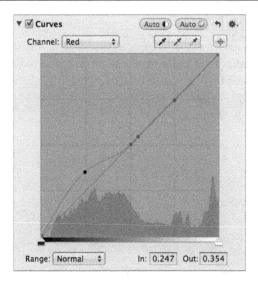

4. If you just want to add reds to your image this is enough, but if you want it to be a more natural warm tone you need to reduce the blue.

5. Switch to the **Blue** channel. Add the three points in the center as per the **Red** channel.

6. Add another point on the first quarter graph lines and drag it down slowly till you get the desired effect.

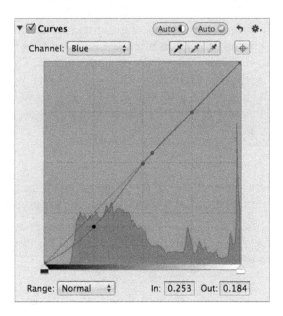

Tinting highlights

To tint the highlights of an image you effectively need to do the same thing in reverse. Instead of adjusting the bottom of the curve, you make your edits at the top. Here is an example of what a curve to cool down the highlights would look like in the following screenshot:

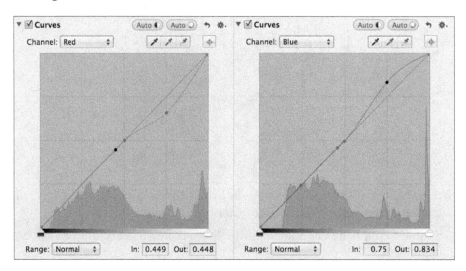

Faded Shadows and Highlights

Another variation of tinting Shadows and Highlights is to create faded shadows or highlights. This is the kind of effect you often see with expired film, and you can use a Curves adjustment to simulate a film-look on your images. The difference between this and the previous method is that this will raise the blacks, whereas the previous method didn't affect the blacks. To give you an example, we will add a faded green look to the shadows. Here's how to do it in the following steps:

1. Start by adding a Curves adjustment to your image.
2. Switch to the **Green** channel.
3. Start by adding a point in the center of the green channel's curve. Add another point at the first quarter where the graph points intersect.
4. Drag the very first point on the curve upwards. Don't add a new point. Use the existing point. Drag it up till it looks like the curve in the following screenshot:

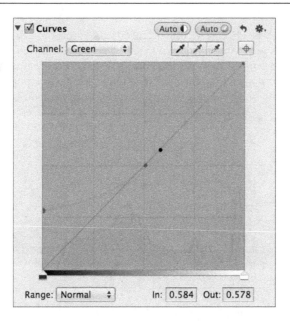

5. You should now have a faded green look to the shadows. You can bring the first point further up to create a more extreme look. You can also add some additional points to give you more control over shadows. For example, if you wanted to limit the effect to only the darkest parts of the shadows, add another point in the lower half of the graph and adjust it till the curve is only going up in the first quarter.

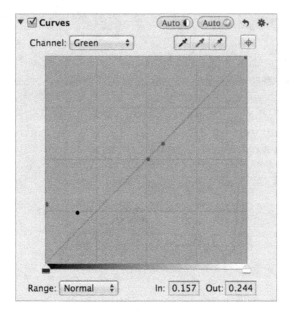

If you want to finely control the curves in the shadow areas of your image, you can zoom in on the shadow area of the curve. From the **Range** pop-up menu at the bottom of the Curves adjustment panel select **Shadows**, as shown in the following screenshot. This will zoom in on the shadows and give you finer control.

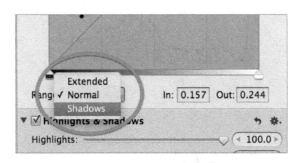

Using the eyedropper and automatic modes

The Curves adjustment has a couple of automatic and semi-automatic modes. It's worthwhile understanding how they work, but in reality, once you have an understanding of Curves, you will find that you rarely use them.

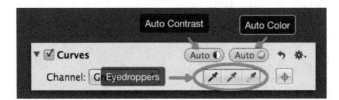

The first set of tools is the **eyedroppers**. If you are familiar with other image editing software, then you are probably familiar with the way these eyedropper tools work. In essence, you select a black point, a white point, and a neutral-gray point in your image and Aperture will adjust the Curves for you accordingly.

Using the eyedroppers

To use the eyedroppers tool carry out the following steps:

1. With a Curves adjustment applied to your image, select the first eyedropper from the three as shown in the previous screenshot. This is the **black point selection** tool.

2. With the eyedropper selected, click on the blackest part of your image, or the area you want to set as black.

3. Now pick the third eyedropper, **White point selection** tool. This will set the white point.

4. Select the area of your image that is the brightest and that you want to be white.

5. Finally select the eyedropper in the middle, which is the **gray point selection** tool. This will set the tone of your image.

6. With the middle eyedropper selected, click on a neutral gray tone in your image. This will now set the colors of your image based on the area you selected.

If you go into the individual channels you will see that the operation has changed all the channels based on what you clicked on. You may find that the results aren't quite what you are looking for so you can either use this as a starting point and tweak the Curves, or start over, and try picking different points of your image.

To reset the Curves adjustment at any time, click on the reset arrow in the top of the curves brick.

Using the automatic adjustments

There are two buttons for automatic adjustments. They work similarly to the eyedropper method, but Aperture automatically sets the levels based on the histogram.

- **Auto Contrast**: The first one only affects brightness and contrast. It won't affect the color of your image.

- **Auto Color**: The second button will set curves for the color channels, but it doesn't affect the main RGB curve.

Extended range Curves

One of the advantages of Aperture's Curves tool over those in other software is that it takes advantage of Aperture's 32-bit architecture and lets you work with values above 100 percent white. This means that if you have values that are clipped, you can use a Curves adjustment to bring the clipped areas back into the visible range. You can also use Curves as an alternative with the **recover** tool.

1. To access the extended range Curves tool, add a Curves adjustment from the **Add Adjustment** pop-up menu, and from the **Range** pop-up menu choose **Extended**.

2. Now you can see the normal range of the curve, which is the visual portion of the image, and also the Curves histogram will show any image data that is above 100 percent.

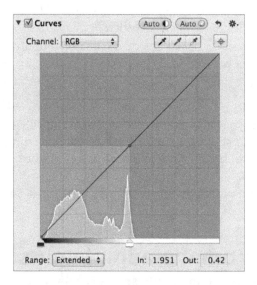

3. If you want to bring this clipped image data back into the visible range, then the process is pretty simple. With a Curves adjustment applied to your image and the **Extended** range mode selected, drag the right-most point until the range of the curve completely encompasses the histogram data.

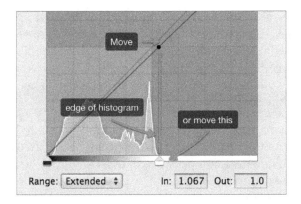

Why would you want to use a Curves adjustment for this rather than just using the recovery slider? Well, there are a few reasons.

- Firstly, with a Curves adjustment, you can control the way the highlights are brought back in, so you can do a nice roll off, creating a more film-like look (see example later in this chapter).

- Secondly, if you have another adjustment that has pushed the value out, you can use Curves to bring it back in. So, for example, if you had turned up the contrast using the contrast slider and your white areas had clipped, you can add an extended range Curves tool to bring the values back into the range. You also might have multiple Curves adjustments and a previous one may have pushed the values too far, so you need a second one to bring them back into visible range.

- Lastly, you can brush a Curves adjustment in, but you can't brush in recovery.

Once you have brought the data back into range you can do whatever you want to the rest of the curve. If you want to add some contrast you can do that, or adjust the brightness in other areas of the image.

Multiple Curves adjustments

Another big advantage of Aperture's Curves tool is that you can have multiple Curves adjustments. If you use this strategically you can save yourself lots of work in the long run. To add a second (and third, fourth, fifth and so on) Curves adjustment, from the cog pop-up menu at the top right of the Curves adjustment panel, choose **Add New Curves Adjustment**.

An example of why you might want to do this is as follows. If you want to add contrast to your image, but you also want to use curves to adjust the colors, rather than doing it in one adjustment, you can do your brightness adjustment in one curve and do the color adjustment in the other. This separates the two processes mentally and will allow you to visualize the adjustments a bit easier. This, in turn, will make it easier to make adjustments.

Another reason is if you need to apply one set of adjustments to one part of an image and one set of adjustments to another. As Curves can be brushed in, you can use multiple Curves adjustments and apply brush masks to them so that they can be limited to areas of the image. This is useful, for example, if you want to darken the skies in an image (see example later in this chapter) or brighten areas of an image. With Curves you get more control than using something like a "dodge and burn", and you get to see what you're doing.

Adding a brush to a Curves adjustment is the same as for any other adjustment. Just choose **Brush Curves In** from the cog menu in the upper-right side of the Curves adjustment panel.

Curves adjustment versus Levels adjustment

If you don't normally use Curves in your adjustments, but instead prefer to use the **levels** tool, you may be wondering what advantage it is to use Curves. There are several reasons to use Curves, but Levels can be very useful too. Aperture's levels tool is actually pretty powerful, and you can do a lot with it. In many ways they both perform the same task, but approach it in different ways. Personally though, I prefer to use the Curves tool.

However, Levels does have a few disadvantages. For a start, you can't access the extended range data with Levels. It only works with the visible range, so you can't use it to recover highlights. You also only have basic control over how the curve is interpolated between points. Another important factor is that, with Curves, you get a very clear visual representation of what you are doing to your image.

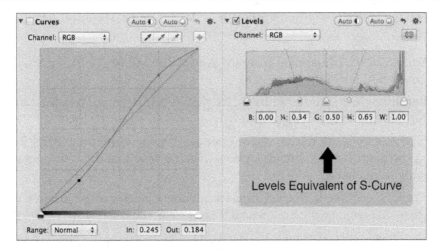

Levels Equivalent of S-Curve

The one big advantage of the levels tool is that it is fairly low-down in the adjustment tree. This means that you can use it to clean up after other adjustments. For example, sometimes you might find that your edits raise the black levels. At that point you can use a Levels adjustment to make sure that the blacks are nicely balanced.

Real world examples

To gain a better understanding of what you can do with Curves, here are some real world examples that will show you how to do a few common tasks with the Curves tool. Hopefully, this will spur your creative juices and allow you to take full advantage of Curves in your own project.

Real world example – darkening skies

Bright skies and dark foreground is a common problem with many types of photography, especially when taking photographs in high-contrast situations. While there are many ways of darkening skies in Aperture, such as the **burn** tool, I personally always prefer to use the Curves tool as it gives the user more control over the process, and excessive use of the burn tool occasionally can cause some odd color shifts.

Select an image with the sky that you want to darken and carry out the following procedure:

1. Add a Curves adjustment from the **Add Adjustment** pop-up-menu in the adjustment tab of the inspector.

2. Start by reducing the brightness. Do this by adding a point in the center of the curve and keep dragging down.

3. Continue to tweak the curves until you're happy with how the sky looks. Ignore the rest of the image for now. Don't worry that the whole image is being darkened.

4. From the cog menu on the Curves adjustment brick choose **Brush Curves in**. This will bring up the brushes HUD and turn your cursor to the brush mode.

5. The image will now revert to its original state without the effect of the Curves adjustment. Carefully brush back in over the sky. This will brush the adjustment you made back in.

6. Once the area is properly brushed, you can go back and make final tweaks to the curves.

Real world example – vignettes

While Aperture has a creative vignette adjustment, it has some limitations too.

- Firstly, it's applied pre-crop, so if you crop your image the vignette may be outside the crop

- Secondly, you have no control over the shape of the vignette, so it is always a basic circular vignette

- Thirdly, it doesn't work very well on portrait-oriented (vertical) images

With the Curves tool and some creative brushing you can make your own vignettes. To do this carry out the following steps:

1. Start by adding a Curves adjustment to an image.

2. Add a point in the center of the curve and drag it down. This should reduce the brightness of the overall image.

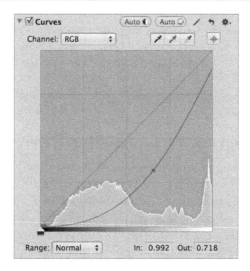

3. From the cog pop-up menu choose **Brush Curves In**. And set the strength on the brush to low.

4. Start slowly and paint on the vignette in the shape you want. Keep the strength low and keep building up the vignette, shrinking the brush each time so as to help smooth the vignettes, edges. If you have a Wacom tablet, you can use your tablet's pen pressure to control the intensity. (Light strokes are needed for this technique.)

5. Switch the brush to feather mode, and smooth out any rough edges or brush artifacts.

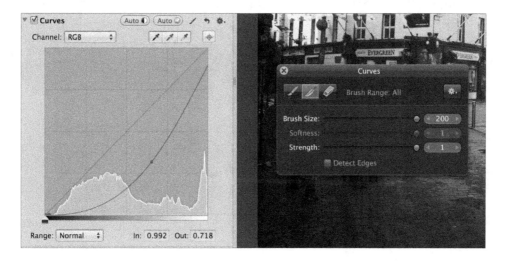

It can be difficult to create smooth gradients and vignettes with the brush tool in Aperture. If you want to make a really smooth vignette, and you are confident enough with some manipulation of the Aperture library, consider using the brush mask editing technique discussed in *Chapter 2, Advanced Adjustments*.

Real world example – controlling highlights

If you have highlights in your image that are quite harsh, you can create a nice soft roll off which mimics the look of a film. This can create a pleasing effect especially if highlights are quite harsh to begin with. This works best on RAW files but will work with JPEG files too. For the purpose of this example, it is assumed that you are going to be using a RAW file. If you are using a JPEG file, you don't need to switch the Curves adjustment to use the extended range. Otherwise the process is the same.

1. Add a Curves adjustment to your image. From the **Range** pop-up menu at the bottom of the adjustment brick choose **Extended** Range.

2. Add a control point in the center of the curve, and another in the third quarter.

3. Drag the point that is the top of the graph over until it encompasses the whole of the histogram. You can also drag the white triangle at the bottom of the graph (it controls the white point).

4. Now, add another point between the top two points on the graph and adjust it. Move the points around till you have a nice gentle slope at the top of the curve. If you need to, don't be afraid to move the white point further than the edge of the histogram. Your resulting curve should look something like the following diagram:

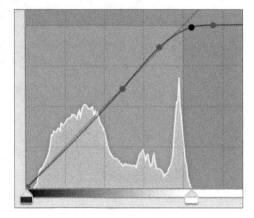

Summary

Hopefully, by now, you will have a thorough understanding of how the Curves adjustment works, and the ways in which you can use it. You will have learned how to do some basic brightness and contrast adjustments using Curves, and why and when you should use them instead of the standard sliders. We looked at using Curves to add warmth to an image, and also how to cool it down. We learned how to tint Highlights and Shadows, how to darken skies, and how to use Curves to create a vignette.

This has just been a starting point though. Now that you are armed with the knowledge of how powerful a feature the Curves tool is, you should be able to leverage it. In the following chapter, we will build upon this knowledge as we look at a few real world examples of manipulating images in Aperture.

4
Aperture in Action

In the previous chapters, we have mainly looked at the theory behind how Aperture works and how to use the software's toolset to complete individual tasks. In this chapter, we will put that theory into practice, and take a look at several real world examples of how you can use Aperture, both creatively and to solve problems. The aim of this chapter isn't to cover every possible problem or scenario that you might encounter, but instead to show you how to use the knowledge you have gained from the previous chapters, and put that knowledge into practical use. The goal is also to help you think outside the box and you may actually be surprised at just how much you can achieve within the software without having to jump over to another application, such as Photoshop.

In this chapter, we will look at the following examples of using Aperture:

- Recovering and controlling clipped highlights
- Fixing blown out skies
- Removing objects from a scene
- Fixing dust spots on multiple images
- Fixing chromatic aberration
- Fixing purple highlight fringes
- Creating fake duotones
- Fix a scanned negatives

Controlling clipped highlights

The problem of clipped highlights is a very common issue that a photographer will often have to deal with. Digital cameras only have limited dynamic range, so clipping becomes an issue, especially with high-contrast scenes. However, if you shoot RAW, then your camera will often record more highlighted information than is visible in the image. You may already be familiar with recovering highlights by using the recovery slider in Aperture, but there are actually a couple of other ways that you can bring this information back into range.

The three main methods of controlling lost highlights in Aperture are:

- Using the recovery slider
- Using curves
- Using shadows and highlights

For many cases, using the recovery slider will be good enough, but the recovery slider has its limitations. Sometimes it still leaves your highlights looking too bright, or it doesn't give you the look you wish to achieve. The other two methods mentioned give you more control over the process of recovery. If you use a **Curves** adjustment, you can control the way the highlight rolls off, and you can reduce the artificial look that clipped highlights can give your image, even if technically the highlight is still clipped. A highlights & shadows adjustment is also useful because it has a different look, as compared to the one that you get when using the recovery slider. It works in a slightly different way, and includes more of the brighter tones of your image when making its calculations. The highlights and shadows adjustment has the added advantage of being able to be brushed in.

So, how do you know which one to use? Consider taking a three-stepped approach. If the first step doesn't work, move on to the second, and so on. Eventually, it will become second nature, and you'll know which way will be the best by just looking at the photograph.

Step 1

Use the recovery slider. Drag the slider up until any clipped areas of the image start to reappear. Only drag the slider until the clipped areas have been recovered, and then stop. You may find that if your highlights are completely clipped, you may need to drag the slider all the way to the right, as per the following screenshot:

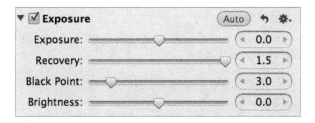

For most clipped highlight issues, this will probably be enough. If you want to see what's going on, add a **Curves** adjustment and set the **Range** field to the **Extended** range. You don't have to make any adjustments at this point, but the histogram in the **Curves** adjustment will now show you how much image data is being clipped, and how much data that you can actually recover.

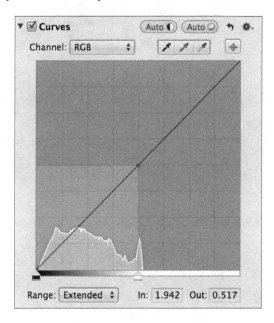

Real world example

In the following screenshot, the highlights on the right-hand edge of the plant pot have been completely blown out:

If we zoom in, you will be able to see the problem in more detail.

As you can see, all the image information has been lost from the intricate edge of this cast iron plant pot. Luckily this image had been shot in RAW, and the highlights are easily recovered.

In this case, all that was necessary was the use of the recovery slider. It was dragged upward until it reached a value of around 1.1, and this brought most of the detail back into the visible range.

As you can see from the preceding image, the detail has been recovered nicely and there are no more clipped highlights. The following screenshot is the finished image after the use of the recovery slider:

Step 2

If the recovery slider brought the highlights back into range, but still they are too bright, then try the **Highlights & Shadows** adjustment. This will allow you to bring the highlights down even further. If you find that it is affecting the rest of your image, you can use brushes to limit the highlight adjustment to just the area you want to recover.

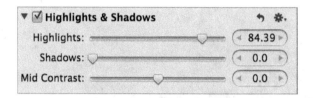

You may find that with the **Highlight and Shadows** adjustment, if you drag the sliders too far the image will start to look flat and washed out. In this case, using the mid-contrast slider can add some contrast back into the image. You should use the mid-contrast slider carefully though, as too much can create an unnatural image with too much contrast.

Step 3

If the previous steps haven't addressed the problem to your satisfaction, or if the highlight areas are still clipped, you can add a roll off to your **Curves** adjustment. We covered this in the previous chapter, but the following is a quick refresher on what to do:

1. Add a **Curves** adjustment, if you haven't already added one.
2. From the pop-up range menu at the bottom of the **Curves** adjustment, set the range to **Extended**.
3. Drag the white point of the **Curves** slider till it encompasses all the image information.
4. Create a roll off on the right-hand side of the curve, so it looks something like the following screenshot (see the previous chapter):

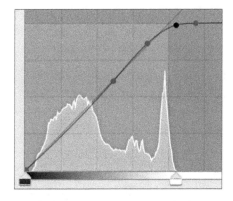

If you're comfortable with curves, you can skip directly to step 3 and just use a **Curves** adjustment, but for better results, you should combine the preceding differing methods to best suit your image.

Real world example

In the following screenshot (of yours truly), the photo was taken under poor lighting conditions, and there is a badly blown out highlight on the forehead:

Before we fix the highlights, however, the first thing that we need to do is to fix the overall white balance, which is quite poor. In this case, the easiest way to fix this problem is to use the Aperture's clever skin tone white-balance adjustment.

On the **White Balance** adjustment brick from the pop-up menu, set the mode to **Skin Tone**. Now, select the color picker and pick an area of skin tone in the image. This will set the white balance to a more acceptable color. (You can tweak it more if it's not right, but this usually gives satisfactory results.)

The next step is to try and fix the clipped highlight. Let's use the three-step approach that we discussed earlier. We will start by using the recovery slider. In this case, the slider was brought all the way up, but the result wasn't enough and leaves an unsightly highlight, as you can see in the following screenshot:

The next step is to try the **Highlight & Shadows** adjustment. The highlights slider was brought up to the mid-point, and while this helped, it still didn't fix the overall problem. The highlights are still quite ugly, as you can see in the following screenshot:

Finally, a **Curves** adjustment was added and a gentle roll off was applied to the highlight portion of the curve. While the burned out highlight isn't completely gone, there is no longer a harsh edge to it. The result is a much better image than the original, with a more natural-looking highlight as shown in the following screenshot:

Finishing touches

To take this image further, the face was brightened using another **Curves** adjustment, and the curves was brushed in over the facial area. A vignette was also added. Finally, a skin softening brush was used over the harsh shadow on the nose, and over the edges of the halo on the forehead, just to soften it even further. The result is a much better (and now useable) image than the one we started with.

Fixing blown out skies

Another common problem one often encounters with digital images is blown out skies. Sometimes it can be as a result of the image being clipped beyond the dynamic range of the camera, whereas other times the day may simply have been overcast and there is no detail there to begin with. While there are situations when the sky is too bright and you just need to bring the brightness down to better match the rest of the scene, that is easily fixed and we covered how to do that in *Chapter 3, Everything you Ever Wanted to Know about Curves*. But what if there is no detail there to recover in the first place? That scenario is what we are going to look at in the next section. This covers what to do when the sky is completely gone and there's nothing left to recover.

There are options open to you in this case. The first is pretty obvious. Leave it as it is. However, you might have an image that is nicely lit otherwise, but all that's ruining it is a flat washed-out sky. What would add a nice balance to an image in such a scenario is some subtle blue in the sky, even if it's just a small amount. Luckily, this is fairly easy to achieve in Aperture. Perform the following steps:

1. Try the steps outlined in the previous section to bring clipped highlights back into range. Sometimes simply using the recovery slider will bring clipped skies back into the visible range, depending on the capabilities of your camera. In order for the rest of this trick to work, your highlights must be in the visible range.

2. If you have already made any enhancements using the **Enhance** brick and you want to preserve those, add another **Enhance** brick by choosing **Add New Enhance adjustment** from the cog pop-up on the side of the interface.

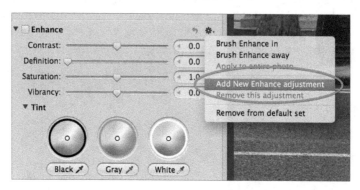

3. If the **Tint** controls aren't visible on the **Enhance** brick, click on the little arrow beside the word *Tint* to reveal the **Tint** controls.

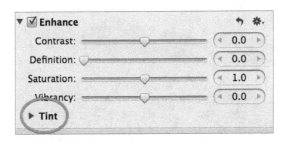

4. Using the right-hand **Tint** control (the one with the **White** eyedropper under it), adjust the control until it adds some blue back to the sky.

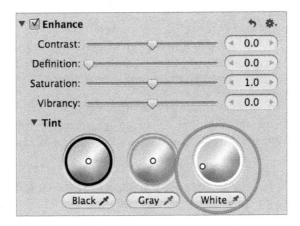

5. If this is adding too much blue to other areas of your image, then brush the enhance adjustment in by choosing **Brush Enhance In** from the cog pop-up menu.

Real world example

In this example, the sky has been completely blown out and has lost most of its color detail. The first thing to try is to see whether any detail can be recovered by using the recovery slider. In this case, some of the sky was recovered, but a lot of it was still burned out. There is simply no more information to recover.

The next step is to use the tint adjustment as outlined in the instructions. This puts some color back in the sky and it looks more natural. A small adjustment of the **Highlights & Shadows** also helps bring the sky back into the range.

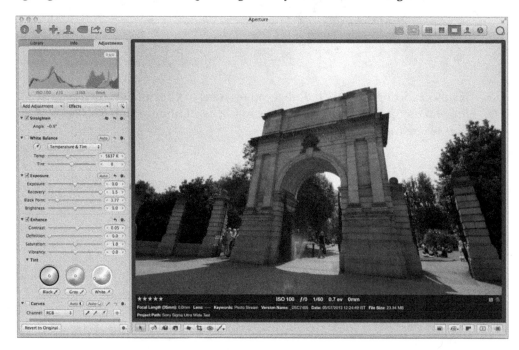

Finishing touches

While the sky has now been recovered, there is still a bit of work to be done. To brighten up the rest of the image, a **Curves** adjustment was added, and the upper part of the curve was brought up, while the shadows were brought down to add some contrast. (See *Chapter 3, Everything you Ever Wanted to Know about Curves*)

The following is the **Curves** adjustment that was used:

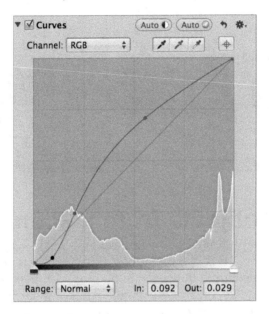

Finally, to reduce the large lens flare in the center of the image, I added a color adjustment and reduced the saturation and brightness of the various colors in the flare. I then painted the color adjustment in over the flare, and this reduced the impact of it on the image. This is the same technique that can be used for getting rid of color fringing, which will be discussed later in this chapter.

The following screenshot is the final result:

Removing objects from a scene

One of the myths about photo workflow applications such as Aperture is that they're not good for pixel-level manipulations. People will generally switch over to something such as Photoshop if they need to do more complex operations, such as cloning out an object. However, Aperture's retouch tool is surprisingly powerful. If you need to remove small distracting objects from a scene, then it works really well. The following is an example of a shot that was entirely corrected in Aperture:

It is not really practical to give step-by-step instructions for using the tool because every situation is different, so instead, what follows is a series of tips on how best to use the retouch function:

- To remove complex objects you will have to switch back and forth between the cloning and healing mode. Don't expect to do everything entirely in one mode or the other.

- To remove long lines, such as the telegraph wires in the preceding example, start with the healing tool. Use this till you get close to the edge of an object in the scene you want to keep. Then switch to the cloning tool to fix the areas close to the kept object.

- The healing tool can go a bit haywire near the edges of the frame, or the edges of another object, so it's often best to use the clone tool near the edges.

- Remember when using the clone tool that you need to keep changing your clone source so as to avoid leaving repetitive patterns in the cloned area. To change your source area, hold down the *option* key, and click on the image in the area that you want to clone from.

Healing too close to an edge

- Sometimes doing a few smaller strokes works better than one long, big stroke.

- You can only have one retouch adjustment, but each stroke is stored separately within it. You can delete individual strokes, but only in the reverse order in which they were created. You can't delete the first stroke, and keep the following ones if for example, you have 10 other strokes.

It is worth taking the time to experiment with the retouch tool. Once you get the hang of this feature, you will save yourself a lot of time by not having to jump to another piece of software to do basic (or even advanced) cloning and healing.

Fixing dust spots on multiple images

A common use for the retouch tool is for removing sensor dust spots on an image. If your camera's sensor has become dirty, which is surprisingly common, you may find spots of dust creeping onto your images. These are typically found when shooting at higher f-stops (narrower apertures), such as f/11 or higher, and they manifest as round dark blobs. Dust spots are usually most visible in the bright areas of solid color, such as skies.

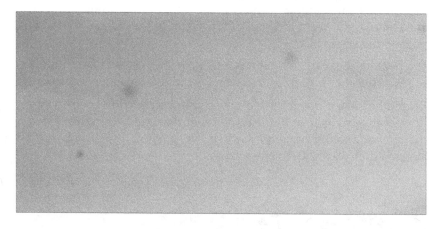

The big problem with dust spots is that once your sensor has dust on it, it will record that dust in the same place in every image. Luckily Aperture's tools makes it pretty easy to remove those dust spots, and once you've removed them from one image, it's pretty simple to remove them from all your images. To remove dust spots on multiple images, perform the following steps:

1. Start by locating the image in your batch where the dust spots are most visible.

2. Zoom in to 1:1 view (100 percent zoom), and press *X* on your keyboard to activate the retouch tool.

3. Switch the retouch tool to healing mode and decrease the size of your brush till it is just bigger than the dust spot. Make sure there is some softness on the brush.

4. Click once over the spot to get rid of it. You should try to click on it rather than paint when it comes to dust spots, as you want the least amount of area retouched as possible.

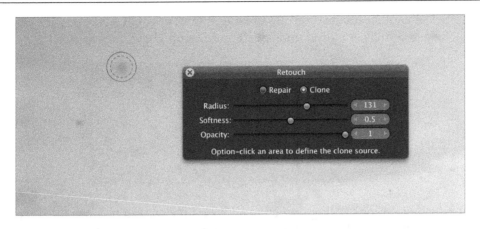

5. Scan through your image when viewing at 1:1, and repeat the preceding process until you have removed all the dust spots

6. Close the retouch tool's HUD to drop the tool. Zoom back out.

7. Select the lift tool from the **Aperture** interface (it's at the bottom of the main window).

8. In the lift and stamp HUD, delete everything except the **Retouch** adjustment in the **Adjustments** submenu. To do this, select all the items except the retouch entry, and press the *delete* (or *backspace*) key.

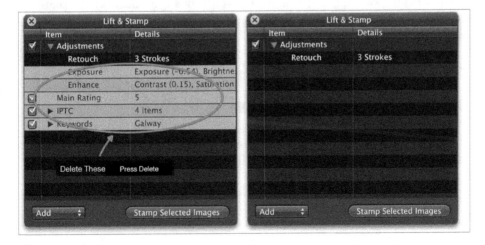

9. Select another image or group of images in your batch, and press the **Stamp Selected Images** button on the **Lift and Stamp** HUD.

Your retouched settings will be copied to all your images, and because the dust spots don't move between shots, the dust should be removed on all your images.

Tips for fixing chromatic aberration

Chromatic aberration is one of the most common image problems, and also one of the easiest to fix. Aperture has a special tool for fixing chromatic aberration, coincidentally called **Chromatic Aberration**.

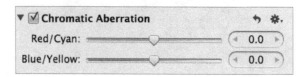

Using it is actually fairly straightforward, so you may be wondering why it is featured here, but there are actually a few tricks that can make it a bit easier to work with when working on multiple images. What follows is a selection of tip and tricks for using the chromatic aberration tool:

- Always zoom in to 1:1 when fixing chromatic aberration, as you can't see the results properly when zoomed out.

- Chromatic aberration is always worst at the edges of the frame. When zooming in to adjust for it, always pan to the edge of the frame. A corner is even better.

- **Red/Cyan** is more common, so always start with that first. This will more often than not remove the chromatic aberration from the shot.

- Depending on the lenses you use regularly, you may have to use this tool on every shot. To make your life easier, add this to the default set of adjustments using the steps outlined in *Chapter 2, Advanced Adjustments*.

- Chromatic aberration varies depending on the lens, the aperture, and if it's a zoom lens, the focal length. Because of this, there's no point in trying to save this as a preset. However, if you regularly use the same lens and it is a prime (or you shoot at the same focal length), then you can use presets to build up a collection of quick fixes for chromatic aberration.

- Remember though, it will only work with images shot using the same aperture. So, you will need to create separate presets for each of the f-stops you generally shoot at, for that specific lens. Your chromatic aberration fix for f/2.8 for example, will be different from the fix for f/8. You could name these presets something along the lines of what follows, so that they are easier to remember and find again later. The following is just an example:

  ° 50 mm Lens f/1.8 CA Fix
  ° 50 mm Lens f/2.8 CA Fix
  ° 50 mm Lens f/8 CA Fix

Fixing purple fringing

Purple fringing is another common problem that you will encounter in digital photography. It's caused by the optical design of a lens, and is different from the standard chromatic aberration. Purple fringing is typically found around bright highlights, and can usually be seen around shiny points on metal. It's also common on water highlights, and it is usually worse on less expensive or poorer quality lenses. It still does present itself on expensive and high-end glass, however. Aperture does have a tool for fixing this problem called the **Halo Reduction** brush, but it's not very good. There is, however, another relatively simple way to fix purple fringing using some of the other tools in Aperture. The following steps explain what to do:

1. With an image that is experiencing the color fringing problem, the first thing to do is zoom in to 1:1 so you can get a better look at what's happening. You may need to make some fine adjustments, so zooming in is essential to see the problem in detail. Once you have zoomed in, pan to an area where the artifacts are most visible.

2. Add a **Color** adjustment to your adjustment stack. If you are already using a **Color** adjustment on your image, add another.

3. If the **Color** adjustment is in compact view, switch to expanded view by pressing the **Expanded View** button, which is the first button of the group of three, which are located on the top right-hand corner of the **Color** adjustment brick (see the following screenshot).

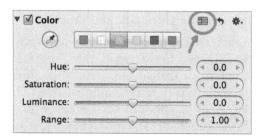

4. Start by dragging down the **Saturation** slider on the purple section of the color slider. Drag it all the way to zero.

5. You may also need to reduce the red slider. Keep an eye on the image while you are making adjustments. You want to do the minimum amount of correcting necessary to remove the artifacts. Once the fringing is gone, you can stop.

6. If the problem is on bright water highlights, you may also need to reduce the **Saturation** slider of the blue and the cyan areas. You will need to judge this by using eyes only, and through trial and error. You will be able to see when you have done enough.

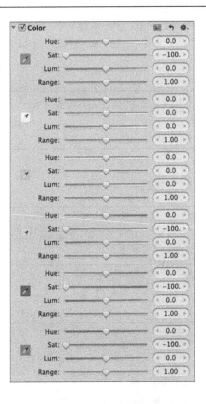

7. Once you have finished adjusting the sliders in the **Color** adjustment brick, and the fringing is gone, zoom back out to double check that you haven't missed anything. The big problem with this technique is that you would have affected the color significantly in the rest of the image. Don't worry about this for now though, as we'll fix that in the next step.

8. To ensure that only the area with the fringing is treated with this effect, add a brush to the **Color** adjustment brick by choosing **Brush Color in** from the cog pop-up menu in the **Color** adjustment brick.

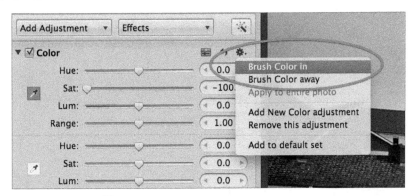

9. Brush over the areas where the fringing is a problem with a soft-edged brush. This should now get rid of the fringing without affecting the rest of the image.

This technique should give you a much more pleasing result than the **Halo Reduction** brush, because the **Halo Reduction** brush is preset to only remove certain colors. Personally, I often find that it also alters the surrounding color too much and it doesn't create a realistic or natural result. By using a brushed color adjustment you have much more control over the result.

Real world example

In the preceding image there is a substantial amount of color fringing in the waterfall. If you zoom in, you can see the problem in more detail.

As you can see in the preceding screenshot, the fringing is a major issue. Luckily, it is easy to fix. Using the settings in the previous section, a **Color** adjustment brick was added and this was then brushed in over the waterfall area.

The result is the following image, free of the color-fringing problem:

Finishing touches

To finish the image and make it a little more interesting, there was some warmth added, as well as some contrast, using a **Curves** adjustment (see *Chapter 3, Everything you Ever Wanted to Know about Curves*). A slight vignette was also added to bring the focus of the image into the waterfall. The following image is the final result:

Creating fake duotones

One of the features notably lacking from Aperture's toolset is a duotone adjustment. A duotone is a halftone printing process made using two inks, usually black and another color. In the digital darkroom, a similar effect is created by tinting the shadows with one color and the highlights with another. While not technically a duotone, this is often a creative choice for photographers looking to create a stylized image. Many applications have a tool specifically for this technique included, but unfortunately Aperture doesn't. You can create sepia images easily enough, but there's no faux duotone effect included in the default toolset. Luckily, you can achieve similar results fairly easily by combining a few different adjustments as shown in the following steps:

1. In the **Enhance** adjustment, set the **Saturation** slider of your image to zero.

2. Add a second **Enhance** adjustment, by choosing **Add New Enhance Adjustment** from the cog pop-up menu.

3. Expand the **Tint** controls if they are hidden.

4. Use the shadow tint control to add color to the shadows. You can control the intensity by how far you move the control away from the center of the color wheel.

5. Use the highlight color control to tint the highlights and add color to the lighter part of the image. Depending on the tonality of the image, you may need to adjust the **Gray** color wheel too.

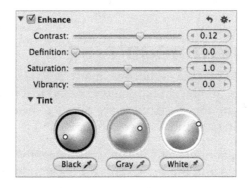

That's pretty much all there is to it. If you find that the intensity of the duotone effect is not strong enough, add a third **Enhance** adjustment brick. You can then use the **Saturation** slider to increase the saturation of the duotone colors.

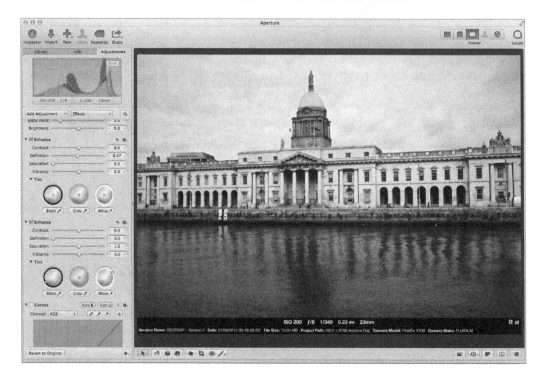

Fixing scanned negatives

Despite the fact that we live in the digital age, many people still use film. The popularity of Holga Cameras, in particular, has led to a renewed interest to store and catalogue images from film. Also, there are plenty of people who have old film negatives (and slides) lying around with which they want to do something.

If you want to sort and catalogue your positives and negatives in Aperture, the first step is to get them scanned and imported. There are a couple of options for doing this. You can have a lab do them for you, which is the easiest option. If you have a film scanner, you can scan them yourself. The third method that some people use, while not ideal, is to use a digital camera and either a macro lens on a light box, or a special holder designed for mounting slides on the end of a lens. If you are using a macro lens and a light box, you need to use some kind of stand to hold your camera steady, and at right angles to the light box.

There are also special holders that you can get which allow you to put the negatives or positives on the end of a lens and capture them using your DSLR. This isn't the best way to capture negatives, but some people use this method if they don't have access to a scanner.

Lomography, the people who make the popular Holga range of cameras, have a clever adaptor to turn your smartphone into a film scanner. You can find out about it at their website http://shop.lomography.com/accessories/smartphone-scanner.

While it won't give you professional quality results, if you're shooting a film with one of their plastic cameras, quality is probably not a major concern.

If you are using your own scanner, you will probably not need to do anything special in Aperture because most scanners have a built-in negative option in their software, which will give you a correct result when scanning a negative. However, if by some chance your scanner doesn't have this option, or you are using the digital camera method, then you will need to invert the image so it becomes positive again. Your photo will also need some color correction to compensate for the inherent orange color of negatives. Luckily though, once you have this figured out, it will be pretty much the same for every negative you use so you can save your setup as a preset. Because Aperture doesn't have an invert tool, you need to use curves to invert an image.

The following are the steps for creating the necessary adjustments to use negatives in Aperture:

1. Import your scanned images into Aperture, or if you've used a digital camera, import the images from your memory card.

2. Select an image to work on as the starting point. You can later apply the same effect to all the images.

3. Add a **Curves** adjustment and invert the curve, so that the left-hand (black point) side starts high, and the right-hand side (white point) ends low. The curve should look like the following screenshot:

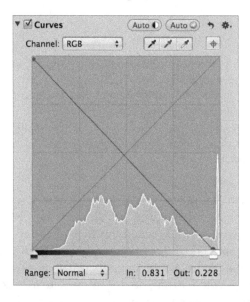

4. Your image should now be looking a bit more normal, although the colors will still look unnatural.

5. Add a second **Curves** adjustment. This is one occasion when using the eyedroppers will help. Select the **black point** eyedropper and click on an area of the image that should be black.

6. Select the **white point** eyedropper and click on an area that should be white.

7. Finally, select the **gray point** eyedropper and click on an area that should be neutral toned.

8. You should now have a reasonably accurate image, but you will probably need to continue to tweak the colors, using both the curves and Aperture's other tools, until you get them right.

9. Finally, you should save your adjustments as a preset. (See Chapter 2, *Advanced Adjustments*). You can now apply this preset to the rest of the images that you have scanned in.

Once you have saved a preset, you should be able to use this as a starting point for every time you want to use negatives in your project again.

 If you are adjusting the exposure of your images after you have applied this negative effect, remember that because your **Curves** adjustment is inverting the image, anything you do in the **Exposure** adjustment brick will have the opposite effect. So, if you increase the **Exposure** slider, it will actually darken your image.

Summary

In this chapter, we built on the theory from the previous chapters to tackle some common real world problems that you may encounter when working with digital images. We looked at the range of tasks you can actually accomplish within aperture, and hopefully you will now have a better understanding of not just how to fix these issues, but how Aperture's advance features can be put to practical use.

In this chapter, everything was without having to go outside the software to achieve the desired results. Sometimes though, you may find that Aperture simply doesn't have the toolset to accomplish what you want it to, and you need to look outside the software. Aperture has a robust plugin architecture, and there are several ways to pair it with third-party applications too. We will cover all this in the next chapter.

5
Extending Aperture

In the previous chapters, we have looked at some of the advanced ways of importing, sorting, and processing the images inside of Aperture, but what if you need to do some editing that you can't achieve within the application itself? Luckily, Aperture has a robust plugin architecture, and a good ecosystem of third-party plugins. It also makes it easy to work with third-party software. In this chapter, we will take a look at how to extend the application. We will look at some essential plugins that every Aperture user should aim to have, and I will also share my favorite third-party tools. We will also take a look at working with third-party RAW converters, at working with Photoshop, as well as some inexpensive Photoshop alternatives.

Aperture's plugin architecture doesn't just support image editing plugins. There are plugins for exporting images to specific services, as well as third-party book modules plugins. However, in this chapter, we will only be looking at image editing plugins, as we will cover export plugins later in the book when we will talk about ways to export images.

In this chapter you will learn about:

- When (and why) you need to go outside Aperture
- What Aperture does when you use a plugin
- Where to find Aperture plugins
- Essential plugins
    - Nik Silver Efex Pro
    - PTLens
    - Color Efex Pro

- Working with external editors
- Working with Photoshop

- Photoshop alternatives
- Using third-party RAW converters
- Working with Lightroom

When and why you need to go outside Aperture

As we have seen in the previous chapters, Aperture is a very powerful piece of software. You can accomplish quite a lot within the application, but it does have its limits. The tools inside Aperture are generally designed for making broad edits to your image, and while you can selectively edit with brushes, if you need to get into precise pixel-level manipulations, you just can't do it within Aperture. So, for example, while we previously looked at how good Aperture's cloning and healing tool is, there are also some limits as to what you can achieve, so for complex edits you may need to use an application, such as Photoshop. There are also some important image correction techniques that Aperture can't do either, or is not very good at. For example, Aperture has no tools for lens distortion correction. For this, you will have to use a plugin. Aperture's noise reduction functionality is also pretty weak compared to its competitors, but there are a few good plugins that offer this functionality.

There are times too, when you may not like the way Aperture converts RAW files from a particular camera, and you might prefer to use a different RAW converter such as the one the manufacturer provides. In this way, you can keep Aperture as a hub that serves to keep all your images together, and you can use it as a jumping-off point for working with other tools. The following are a few common tasks that you may need to accomplish with a plugin, or third-party piece of software:

- Fixing lens distortion
- Noise reduction
- Creative filters
- Working with HDR sequences
- Merging panoramas
- Working with text and layers
- Creating better black and white images
- Complex cloning and airbrushing
- Alternative RAW conversion
- Film emulation
- Enlarging and resizing images
- Restoring damaged or old images

What Aperture does when you use a plugin

When you use a plugin in Aperture or edit an image in an external editor, Aperture has to make a flat copy of your file. This is because of the way your edits in Aperture are stored in a non-destructive recipe, which most third-party software doesn't understand. Also, many plugins will not work with RAW image data (although some do). When you invoke the command to edit with a plugin (by right-control clicking on the image and choosing **Edit in...**). Aperture creates a TIFF or Photoshop PSD version of your image with all your edits baked in. This is then sent to the plugin or the third-party application. When you have finished and exited out of the plugin, this file is then saved, so that when you return to Aperture it is stacked with the original (depending on your preferences).

To have the edited file stack with the original, perform the following steps:

1. Go to the **Preferences** option by navigating to **Aperture | Preferences** from the menu.
2. Select the **General** tab.
3. Tick the checkbox that says **Automatically stack new versions**.

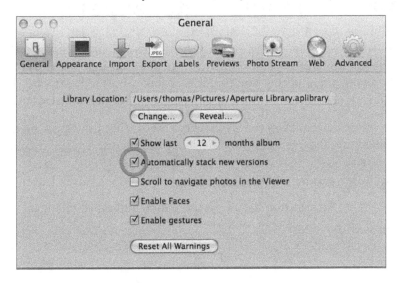

Most of the time you will want this edited image to be the one you want to use, rather than the original RAW file. But when Aperture stacks the edited file with the original, it is often not the pick of the stack, so if you collapse the stack, the original will be the image on top and not the edited version. To make your edited image the pick of the stack, with the image still selected, press *command + *.

Now here's the important part. If you edit that edited image again in another plugin (or even the same plugin), Aperture will save over the edited image. Once you have done this, there is no way to undo it. Therefore, if you want to keep a version of your edited file before editing again, make a new version of your image (and make sure you make a new version of the edited image, not the original.) The only problem with this approach is that each new edited version will use up space on your drive, because Aperture is actually duplicating the file each time. You can always delete the intermediate versions though once you are finished. Alternatively, if you know that you don't need to keep an edited file, just don't create a new version before you invoke the next plugin.

Mountain Lion and Gatekeeper

If you are running Aperture on Mountain Lion (OS X 10.8) or later, you may run into an issue with Mountain Lion's security system called Gatekeeper, and Aperture plugins. If the plugin hasn't been updated to work with Gatekeeper, you may get an error when you run it, telling you that it is an unauthorized software. To fix this issue, you may need to disable Gatekeeper by performing the following steps:

1. Go to your System Preferences by choosing it from the Apple menu, or by launching the System Preferences app from your `Applications` folder in the finder.

2. Click on the **Security & Privacy** button.

3. Click on the **lock** button to unlock the panel, and make changes.

4. Enter your password.

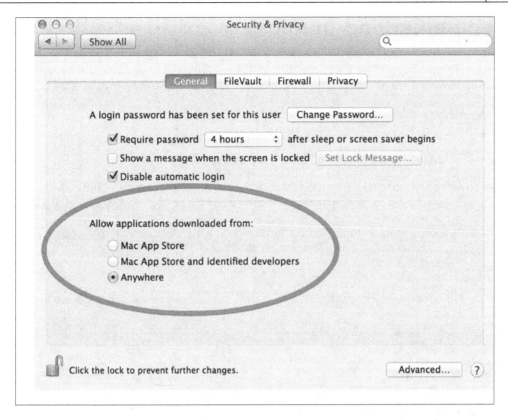

5. Under the section called **Allow applications downloaded from**, click on the button that says **Anywhere**. This should solve the problem, however, be aware that your computer could now potentially run malware. However, this is no different than how your computer would have behaved before Mountain Lion was released.

Where to find plugins

There are quite a few plugins available for Aperture. In the following sections, we will look at what I consider to be essential plugins, as well as some other common add-ons. However, if you want to see what is available, Apple maintains a page of third-party resources for Aperture. You can find it by visiting the following website:

http://www.apple.com/aperture/resources/plugins.html

Recommended plugins

There are a few plugins that every Aperture owner should aim to get (depending on finances of course). While there are lots of other great tools available, in my opinion, these few are the most useful and important. They are the following:

- PTLens
- Silver Efex Pro (part of the Nik Software Suite)
- Dfine (also part of the Nik Software Suite)

They aren't very expensive, especially PTLens. Silver Efex Pro and Dfine are part of the one suite of tools, which also includes the excellent Color Efex Pro and Viveza.

Let's have a look at each of these and understand why they are so important.

PTLens

- Developed by ePaperPress, $25, http://epaperpress.com/ptlens/

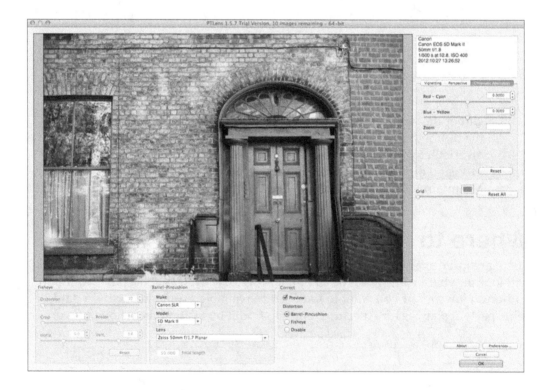

PTLens does one thing, but it does it very well. It fixes lens distortion. The software comes with a large database of lenses, and it has the distortion characteristics of those lenses mapped out. When you use the plugin, it will look at the metadata of your file to see what lens you took the shot with, and if it is in its database, it applies the necessary geometric correction corresponding to that lens.

Lens correction is a really important feature and it is something that many users of Aperture have long wished to be included in the software. Most other modern RAW converters actually have this kind of lens correction built in, so it's a shame Aperture doesn't yet have this feature. Luckily though, PTLens does a really good job and is quite inexpensive.

Many camera and lens manufactures rely on software within the camera to correct for lens distortion, but when you open up the RAW file that distortion correction is lost. It is especially apparent on wide-angle lenses. Without lens correction, you can have strongly distorted curves where there should be straight lines. With PTLens you can correct that and solve these issues. The following is an example of an image which had strong distortion that was corrected by using PTLens:

In the preceding example, you can see how the bowed lines of the river wall were taking away from an otherwise strong composition. This was fixed in PTLens in a matter of seconds.

To use PTLens, first download the software, and then follow the instructions for installation. They offer a 15-day trial version, so if you want to try it out before buying, you can do so.

1. Inside Aperture, invoke the plugin by right-control clicking on an image, and navigating to **Edit with Plugin | PTLens**.

2. When the window opens up, if your lens is recognized, the correct correction is automatically applied.

3. If it is not applied, select your camera make and model from the pop-up menus, and select your lens.

4. Click on **OK** when done. This will save the image back out to Aperture.

You can do much more with this plugin. You can correct for both perspective and fisheye distortion, and you can also correct for chromatic aberration within the software too. The company's website has some tutorials on using the full functionality of the plugin, but for basic lens correction, the procedure is as simple as previously outlined.

Silver Efex Pro

- Nik Software / Google, part of the Nik Plugin Suite, $149,
  http://www.niksoftware.com/nikcollection/usa/intro.html

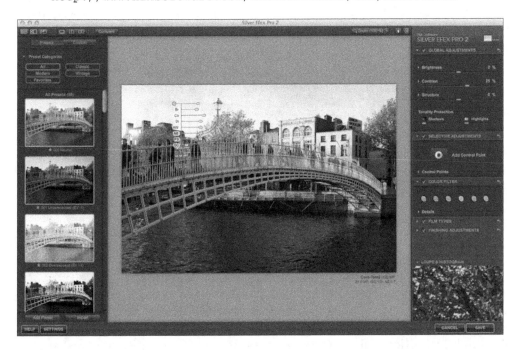

Silver Efex Pro is part of an excellent set of plugins for Aperture (and Lightroom and Photoshop) from Nik Software. The individual plugins in the suite used to be available as individual purchases, but last year Google bought the company that makes them, and it now offers the complete collection for just $149. You used to pay around this for the individual tools within the suite. In fact, they used to sell the collection for $499, so it is a substantial reduction and well worth it.

Silver Efex Pro is a plugin for creating black and white conversions. That may not sound like much, but it does it extremely well. It was engineered to mimic the look you can get from black and white prints that were created using traditional techniques, and the old silver halide technology is where it got its name from. The results can be quite stunning, and although it just creates black and white images, it's actually a pretty powerful tool in its own right.

A quick tour of Silver Efex Pro

Once you launch the plugin, you're greeted with the three-pane interface of Silver Efex Pro. On the left is a collection of presets that you can use to quickly create a black and white look for your images. In the center is the main image view, and on the right are the controls for creating and tweaking your look.

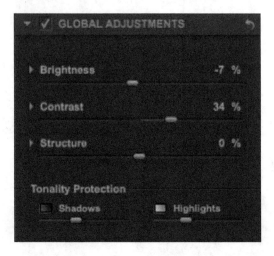

At the top of the control pane is a section for global controls. There you can add contrast, adjust the exposure, and add structure. **Structure** is like a cross between Aperture's **Definition** slider and a sharpness control. It adds micro contrast and sharpness in a unique way, and if applied sparingly, it can be quite effective at adding details to your scene. You can control how the effects are applied to the shadows and highlights in this section too, meaning you can roll the effect off nicely, to prevent clipping in both the whites and the blacks.

Following the global controls is the section for selectively adjusting your image. Like all of Nik's plugins, Silver Efex Pro uses Nik's **U-Point** control system. This is a very clever way to selectively control your scene. With the U-Point system, you add a control point to your scene, placing it over the area you want to adjust. The control point has a radius that you can set. This radius controls the distance from the control point that is affected by your adjustments, and it falls off softly to that radius. It's cleverer than that though, because it knows what part of the scene the control point is over, and it affects only similar areas. It is as if it is performing a luminance key on the image, based on the area you have positioned the point on, and it falls off to a circle based on the radius.

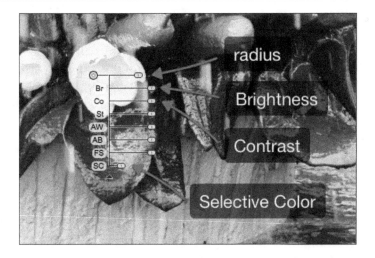

Each control point has a set of controls attached to it. Adjusting these mini sliders lets you control the brightness, contrast, and structure. It also has controls for fine structure, and a very useful slider that allows you to add the color, under the control point back into your image. This allows you to create those nice effects, where an image is monochrome except for one strong color.

Following the selective controls, on the right-hand panel is the color filter section. There you can add a virtual color filter, mimicking the effect of adding a color filter to the front of your lens in traditional black and white film photography. Following this, you can set a selection of film stocks and control the film response curve. Following that are the controls for adding a vignette and for darkening the edges of an image. There is also an option for adding creative edges to your image with effects ranging from the typical film frame edges to brushed and torn-edge effects.

As you can see, there are a lot of options in this seemingly simple plugin, and you could fill a whole chapter with advice and techniques for using this alone. The combination of the innovative U-Point control system, and the film and filter controls, allow you to make some very creative black and white images.

Dfine

- Nik Software / Google, part of the Nik Plugin Suite, $149, http://www. niksoftware.com/nikcollection/usa/intro.html

Dfine is another one of those tools that does one thing, but does it very well. Dfine is for reducing image noise. That's all it does. It samples your image, and based on its analysis, it will reduce both color and luminance noise. You can let it run in fully automatic mode, or you can manually tell it where to sample and profile your image from. You can also control the amount of noise reduction, with separate controls for both the luminance and color noise reduction. The plugin also uses Nik's U-Point technology to allow you to selectively control the noise reduction should you need to increase or decrease the effect in various parts of the image.

If you are wondering why you need to use a plugin for noise reduction, as Aperture has noise reduction built in, the reason is simple. Dfine is far superior at reducing noise in an image, compared to Aperture's default controls. It's as simple as that. If you shoot a lot of high ISO photography, and need to reduce the noise, then Dfine will do a much better job of the task than Aperture alone will ever do.

Honorable mentions

There are a number of other great image editing plugins for Aperture that are worth having, but that aren't what I would consider to be essential. The following are a few that I personally recommend and use on a regular basis:

Color Efex Pro

- Nik Software / Google, part of the Nik Plugin Suite, $149, http://www. niksoftware.com/nikcollection/usa/intro.html

You might be tempted to think of Color Efex Pro as a color film version of Silver Efex Pro, but it is actually a whole suite of filters that you can apply to your images in Aperture, without having to go to an application, such as Photoshop. There is a large selection of filters included within the plugin, and they cover things such as gradient filters to detail enhancing effects. There is also a really great vignette tool in the software, and it also has some basic film grain as well as some film simulation effects.

One of the great things about Color Efex Pro is that you can stack multiple filters together, and you can control how they are applied, and to what section of your image using Nik's control point technology. You can also save sets of filters as recipes for later reuse. Many of the filters actually address some of Aperture's shortcomings. There is a comprehensive graduated filter selection with fairly extensive controls, and the vignette tool is also much better than Aperture's. The other great thing about it is that if you get Silver Efex Pro, you will get Color Efex Pro too as they are all part of the same bundle.

Photomatix

- HDR Soft $119 for bundle / $79 for standalone plugin, http://www.hdrsoft.com/download.html

Photomatix is a tool for creating HDR images from either a single image or a series of bracketed exposures. While there are a few tools on the market now for creating the HDR images, Photomatix is one of the first, and in this author's humble opinion it is still the best. You can buy the software either as a plugin for Aperture or as a standalone application, or as a bundle with both versions. The standalone version will actually open RAW files and use the extended range data to create an HDR image from the extra information available in the RAW file. With the plugin version, you can send either a single image or a series of bracketed images from Aperture to the plugin, and it will combine them into a single HDR image.

Once your sequence has been converted to an HDR image, you can use tone mapping or dynamic range compression to create a standard image. A tone-mapped image is what people normally think of when they think of an HDR image. An actual HDR file looks like a flat normal image. The tone-mapped version is then sent back to Aperture when you save the file.

 A good alternative to Photomatix is the HDR Efex Pro, which is actually part of the Nik Software Suite, so if you buy any of the Nik plugins, you will also get the HDR Efex Pro.

Working with external editors

Aperture allows you to easily send a file to an external editor, such as Photoshop, and once that file is saved, Aperture will automatically import the resulting file back into your Aperture library (and stack it with the original, if you have the **Automatically stack with original** preference set). This process is generally referred to as round-tripping.

You can only set one external editor at a time, but you can change it as often as you want. As with plugins, when you edit a file in an external editor, Aperture creates a flattened version as a standard image file in either TIFF or Photoshop format. Once you save this file back into Aperture, and if you want to edit it again, you will save over the same file. If you want to keep a separate version, you need to use the **Duplicate Version** command.

Setting external editors preferences

There are some preferences that you need to set before you can work with an external editor, including the obvious one, setting which application you want to use. To access the preferences, navigate to the **Aperture** menu and select **Preferences**. Alternatively, you can use the keyboard shortcut, *command + ,*.

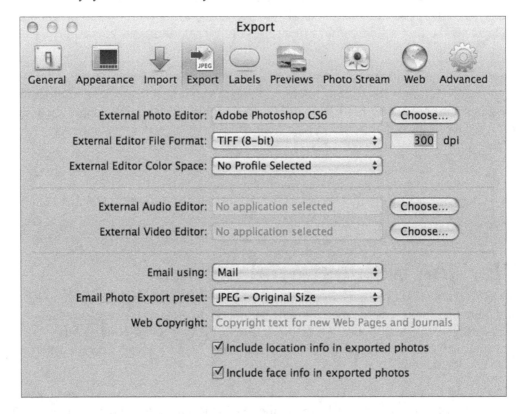

Once you are in the **Preferences** section, click on the **Export** tab. This will bring you to the external editor preferences. Here you can set an external editor for photos, for video, and for audio. For now, we are just concerned with the **External Photo Editor** options.

The first thing that needs to be set is the application you want to use. On the line that says **External Photo Editor**, click on the **Choose...** button. Now, navigate to your Applications folder, and select the application you want to use. This can be Photoshop, obviously, or any other application that works with images. We will discuss some alternatives to Photoshop later in the chapter.

Once you have set your Application, the next most important thing to set is the file format and DPI. Aperture lets you choose, between TIFF and Photoshop (`.psd`) formats in either 8 or 16 bit. You need to choose a format that works with your external editor. Most image editing applications will accept TIFF. If you are using Photoshop, you can select either. TIFF will actually support layers, and Photoshop works well with TIFF, so you can set TIFF, or alternatively use Photoshop format, if you want to ensure the broadest possible compatibility with your potential Photoshop edits.

Whether you choose 8 bit or 16 bit is up to you. 16 bit will preserve the most fidelity of the original file, and will give you the most scope for making advanced color corrections. On the other hand, 16 bit uses up more space, so if space is an issue, 8 bit could be the better option. Personally, I always use 16 bit.

The DPI controls what DPI is set, when you open the file in an external editor. It should be noted though that this doesn't resize the image, it just sets what DPI the file is set at. Some people are confused by this, but just remember that it's not resizing the file, it's just embedding the size the image will be printed at.

The last option is color space. This setting lets you apply a color profile when sending the file to an external editor. If you set it to **No Profile Selected**, it will use the color profile embedded in the image. Alternatively, the best suggestion is to set it to Adobe RGB, as this is the color space that Aperture works in internally.

Working with Photoshop

Photoshop is probably the most common photo editor that people will use with Aperture. Aperture and Photoshop work well together, and Aperture will read and display Photoshop files. However, there are a few things to be aware of when working with Photoshop.

Firstly, while Aperture does support Photoshop files, it doesn't support layers or any of Photoshop's other features. So, while you can see the Photoshop files in Aperture, if it contains layers, all you will see in Aperture is the flattened version of the image.

Secondly, if you save your Photoshop file back to Aperture, and it has an alpha channel in the file, Aperture will display that channel as transparency. This can be problematic, if for example, you are using channels as a temporary mask. When you save Photoshop files back to Aperture, you may be wondering why half the image is missing. An extra channel may well be the culprit. There isn't anything particularly complicated about working with Photoshop though.

Aperture doesn't directly integrate with some of Photoshop's special functionality, such as making panoramas or merging to HDR, but there is a straightforward workaround. What follows is an example of a workflow for quickly creating panoramas in Photoshop, but the same trick will work for other things, such as merging to HDR.

A quick way to create panoramas in Photoshop

If you want to create panoramas by stitching together a number of images, you probably use Photoshop for that task. Unlike Adobe's own Lightroom, Aperture doesn't have the function to send a group of images to Photoshop to be merged. If you do this already, you are probably familiar with the long-winded workflow of exporting your images from Aperture into a special folder, opening them up in Photoshop, and so on. There is however, a quicker way to do this if you're willing to make a small compromise. This trick requires you to use the Aperture previews, so it is important that the preferences are set right to maintain the best image quality when using this method. Let's start by setting the preferences.

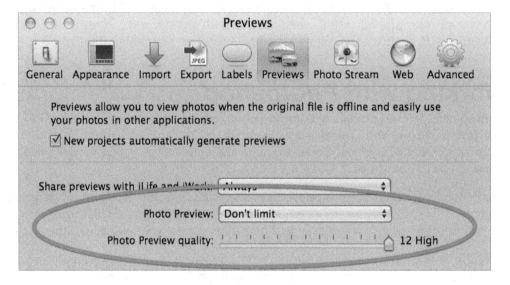

1. From the **Aperture** menu, select **Preferences**, or press *command + ,*.
2. Navigate to the **Previews** tab.
3. Set the pop-up menu for **Photo Preview** to **Don't Limit**.
4. Set **Photo Preview Quality** to **12**.
5. Click on **OK** to exit **Preferences**.

If you have already imported your images, you will need to regenerate previews. To do this, select your images, and right-click on an image, then hold down the *option* key, and select **Generate Previews**.

This will allow you to drag-and-drop images into Photoshop. When you drag-and-drop images from Aperture onto another application or the finder, it uses the previews as the source. The downside of setting your previews to maximum quality is that it uses up more disk space.

Now to create the panorama in Photoshop, perform the following steps:

1. Make sure Photoshop is in your dock, and if you want, you can start Photoshop before continuing so that you're not waiting for it to load.

2. Select the images you want to merge, and drag them onto the Photoshop icon in the dock.

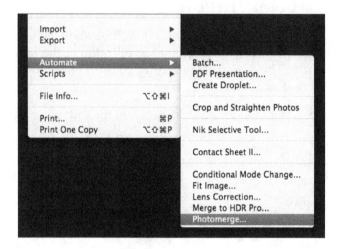

3. In Photoshop, from the menu navigate to **File | Automate | Photomerge....**

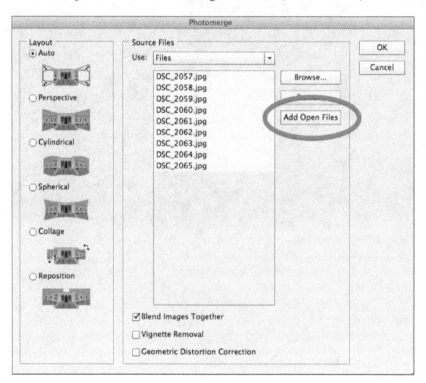

4. In the resulting window, press the button that says **Add Open files**.

5. Set your other options and click on **OK**.

6. Once Photoshop has finished processing, you can save the resulting file and reimport it into Aperture.

Photoshop alternatives

If you can't afford Photoshop or simply don't want to use it, then there are a number of good alternatives in the market at the time of writing this book. They have their advantages and disadvantages. The biggest disadvantage for using software, other than Photoshop, is that Aperture will likely not support the native file formats of these applications. This unfortunately means that you will need to save a flattened version as a TIFF or JPEG, in order for it to be loaded back into Aperture, meaning you will lose any application-specific functions, or even just layers. You could always save a native file to a different location as a back up, but your workflow becomes quite disorganized in that case.

Having said that, there are some great applications out there at the moment, and most of them are relatively inexpensive. In the following pages, we will look at the details of two of the most popular third-party image editing applications in the market right now, and we will examine some of the advantages and disadvantages of each when compared to using Photoshop.

Pixelmator

- Pixelmator Team Ltd, www.pixelmator.com, Mac App Store, $14.99

Pixelmator is a beautifully designed image editing application with a gorgeous user interface. It looks a lot like Photoshop, and has a good deal of Photoshop's functionality with quite a few quirks of its own. It is very fast and uses a lot of OS X's core technologies. The developers are also updating it very regularly, and each update to date has brought considerable new features.

It has many of the key features that you would want as a companion to Aperture, including a nice healing tool, and good cloning and sharpening tools. Pixelmator also has a good set of painting and selection tools, but it lacks channels and the ability to save selections to an alpha channel (although the app does support layer masks). The one thing that is immediately apparent when using Pixelmator though, is the speed. It is very well programmed and makes good use of your computer's **Graphics Processing Unit (GPU)**. I personally have found that you can launch Pixelmator, make simple edits, and save your images in the time Photoshop would have taken to load.

Key advantages

- Very fast
- Quick to load
- Comprehensive tool set
- Modern UI
- Familiar interface for Photoshop users
- Great set of online tutorials for learning the software
- Good selection tools and sharpening tools
- Healing brush
- ColorSync support and soft proofing
- Inexpensive compared to Photoshop
- iCloud support

Disadvantages

- No CMYK color model mode or LAB color mode conversions
- No channels
- Native file format not supported by Aperture
- No actions or built-in automation (does have comprehensive Automator support though)
- Lack of third-party plugins

If you just need to make basic edits, then Pixelmator is a good option. If you're a skilled Photoshop user, this may not be the best tool for you, but then you probably have Photoshop already anyway. They do have a trial version available if you want to try it, and it is very inexpensive so it is worth considering.

Acorn

- Flying Meat Software, `flyingmeat.com/acorn`, Mac App Store, $29.99 (at the time of writing)

Acorn is another modern image editing application for the Mac. It has a more limited toolset than Pixelmator, but it does have one very cool trick up its sleeve. Everything is non-destructive. Any filters that you apply are applied non-destructively, and you can always go back and change an effect, unless you flatten it. It does lack some key functionalities, such as cloning or healing tools, but if you just want to add text and basic filtering or sharpening, this may be an option for you. The software does have a loyal fan base and is highly rated among its users.

Key advantages

- Fast
- Non-destructive editing
- Simple to use
- Layer masks
- Photoshop file support

Disadvantages

- No cloning or healing
- No channel or mode support
- Limited retouching tools
- Native file format not supported by Aperture
- No plugins
- No automation except through Automator or AppleScript

Honourable mention – Photoshop Elements

- Adobe $99, Adobe.com

There is another seemingly obvious alternative to Photoshop and that is its cut-down little brother, Photoshop Elements. It currently sells for $99 directly from Adobe and has many of the features of the full Photoshop. If price is your main issue with Photoshop, then Elements is a possible alternative. However, there are a couple of things to consider. For a start, it's considerably more expensive than Pixelmator, which offers many of the same features. Secondly, since Adobe has switched over to a subscription pricing for its products, you can get the full version of Photoshop for $20 a month. Considering the difference in functionality, and considering that Elements costs $99, it's hard to justify the cost, when for that price, you could get half a year's subscription of the full thing. Still, some people prefer to own their software, so it is an option and it does work well with Aperture.

Working with third-party RAW converters

One of the quirks of the RAW image format is that there can be quite a difference in the interpretation of a file, depending on the RAW converter. The same image can look quite different, depending on the software used to decode it. Aperture does a pretty good job with most RAW files, but your personal preference might be to use a different converter for certain files. For example, if you prefer the RAW conversion from your camera manufacturer's supplied software to Aperture's interpretation, you might want to use that software rather than Aperture for images from that camera. Another possibility is that you may want to use a feature that Aperture doesn't have in its conversion, such as fringing removal or color profile support. You may want to use a third-party converter to enable those functions, but you still want to keep your images in Aperture.

There are a couple of workflow possibilities that you can use to accomplish the task of using a different RAW converter. The most obvious is to import all your files from a shoot into the other software, do all the editing and processing there, then export the selects onto your disk and reimport them into Aperture.

The other option is to import the files into Aperture, and do your rating and selecting in Aperture. You can then just export your selects as originals to disk. Once on disk, you can import them into the RAW software of your choice, process and edit your images, then export them back and reimport them into Aperture.

If this sounds pretty convoluted, you would be right. Luckily, there is a very useful plugin that makes this process a whole lot easier. It's called **Catapult** and it's available at Brushed Pixel.

Catapult

• Brushed Pixel, `brushedpixel.com`, $29, CAD

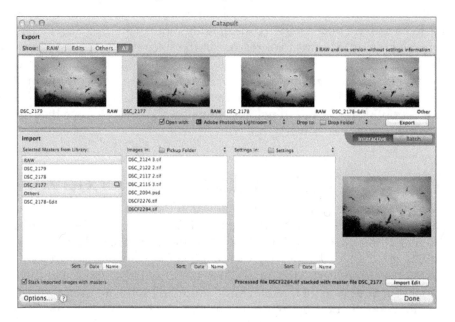

Catapult is a superb plugin for Aperture that automates the process of sending RAW files from Aperture to another application. With Catapult, you can edit a group of images and it will send the RAW files to the application of your choice. It will then watch for edited images in a special folder that it creates. When it detects them (which you have exported back out of your selected RAW processing application), it will import them automatically back into Aperture and stack them with the original images.

If you're wondering what the difference is between using Catapult and just setting the RAW converter as an external editor the big difference is that if you use the external editor function of Aperture, it will only send a TIFF or a PSD file to the application. With Catapult, you can edit the actual RAW file.

Using Catapult

To demonstrate Catapult in use, let's use an example of working with some files from the Fuji X-E1. While Aperture supports files from the X-E1, the software that comes with the camera supports some of the camera's picture profiles, and gives a cosmetically different result to Aperture. This is just an example of course, and this technique will work for any RAW file and for most RAW converters.

1. To start, import and select the images in Aperture like you normally would.

2. Once you have selected the images you want to work with, right-click (or *control* + click) on the **Selection** and navigate to **Edit in | Catapult**.

3. This opens the Catapult interface.

4. First, you need to set the application you want to use to edit your RAW files in. From the option that says **Open with**, use the pop-up menu to select your application. For this example, we are going to use RAW file converter (which is supplied with Fuji's cameras).

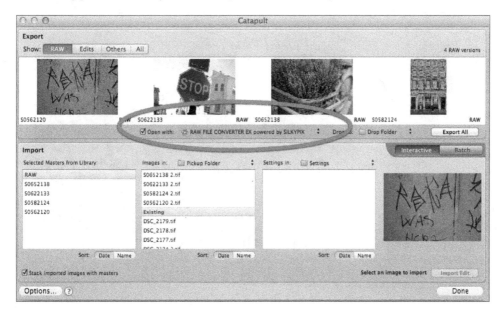

5. When you select the software you want to use, it may launch. Just switch back to Aperture.

6. Click on the **Export All** button.

7. This will send your files to the other software. You may need to manually switch to the software after this is complete.

8. Process your images according to your taste in the other application.

9. Export your images. When exporting, you need to set Catapult's `pickup` folder as the destination. This is found on your desktop, inside the folder called `Catapult Scratch`.

10. Switch back to Aperture.

11. In the Catapult interface, switch to batch mode.

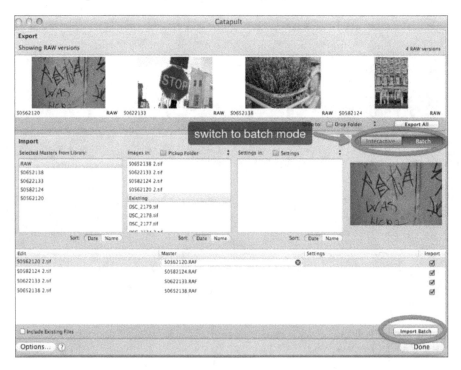

12. Click on the button that says **Import Batch**. This will import the edited files back into Aperture.

13. Click on **Done** to exit the Catapult interface. The edited files should now be back in Aperture.

Catapult will work with most RAW converter software. If you want to use Adobe's Camera Raw to edit your images using Catapult, then you need to set Photoshop as the target application. Because you are passing it RAW files, Photoshop will open them in Camera Raw.

Working with Adobe Photoshop Lightroom

While some hardcore Aperture users might object to the idea of working with Lightroom, it actually has some very useful functions, especially when it comes to processing images. If you want to work mainly with Aperture, but occasionally want to use the editing functionality of Lightroom, there are a few ways to go about it. You could use Catapult, as outlined in the previous section as it works perfectly well with Lightroom. You just have to remember to set the pickup folder as your output destination, when exporting out the images. You can save this as an export preset, so that you can quickly send files back in the future.

If you don't have catapult there is a way to set up a similar workflow using the built-in functionality of Lightroom, and with a little help from OS X's automation tool, Automator. The following is a step-by-step guide for setting up this workflow. It's a little tricky, but once you set it up it's very simple to utilize.

Setting up Lightroom and finder

1. Before we start, we need to set a few things up. Start by going to your finder, and switching to the desktop. On the desktop, create two folders. Call one, Send to Lightroom, and call the other, Send to Aperture.

2. Open Lightroom.

3. From the menu, navigate to **File | Auto Import | Auto Import Settings**.

4. Set the **Watched Folder** field to the Send to Lightroom folder you created earlier.

5. Set the destination to wherever you want Lightroom to store the images.

6. Click on **OK** to exit the dialog.

7. Enable auto import by navigating to **File | Auto Import | Enable Auto Import**.

Now anything you save into the Send to Lightroom folder will be automatically imported into Lightroom's catalog. We could just leave it at that and do everything else manually, but we can make the workflow even easier by setting up some Automator actions. In the following section, we will create two Automator actions. The first one we create will export originals from Aperture to the Send to Lightroom folder with just one click. The second will import the files back to Aperture and allow you to select a project to import them into.

1. Open Automator from your `Applications` folder.

2. When it asks what type of document you want to create, select **Application**.

3. Select photos in the left-most column, and then find the action called **Get Selected Images** with an Aperture icon (make sure it has an Aperture icon).

4. Add this to your workflow.

5. Find the **Export Masters** action with the Aperture icon. Add this to your workflow.

6. Under **Destination** field, set the destination folder to be the `Send to Lightroom` folder you created earlier.

7. U

8. nder the **Utilities** heading in the first column, add the action **Launch Application**. Set Lightroom as the application (this should automatically switch you to Lightroom, when you run the action).

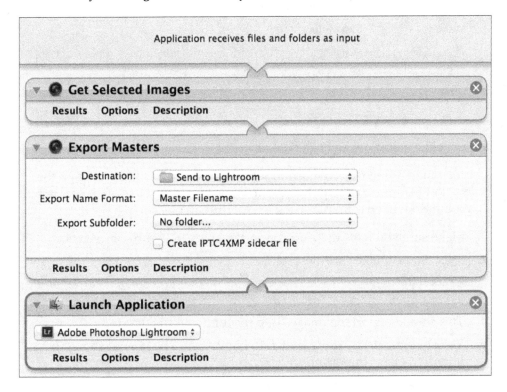

9. Save the workflow and call it `Send to Lightroom`.

10. Add the application to your dock for easy access.

11. Create a new Automator document and again select **Application** as the type.

12. From the photos section of the library, add an **Import Photos** (the one with an Aperture icon) action to the workflow.

13. Click on the workflow's **Options** button at the bottom of the workflow.

14. Tick the option that says, **Show this action when the workflow runs**.

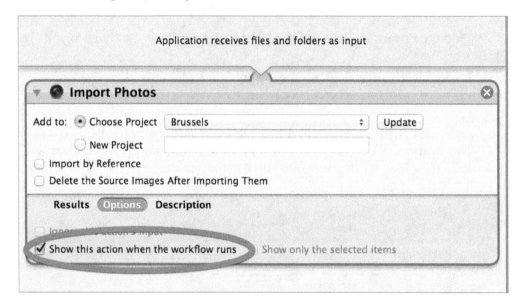

15. Save the workflow and call it `Send to Aperture`.

There is one more thing that we need to set up, but we need to run through the workflow first before we can do that. What we need to do is save an export template in Lightroom, so we can send files back to Aperture in one click.

1. Make sure you have the **Auto Import** enabled in Lightroom.

2. Select some images in Aperture.

3. Launch the `Send to Lightroom` workflow that you created earlier and put in your dock.

4. This should export the images into the folder on the desktop.

5. You should automatically switch to Lightroom. The images should be imported or are importing.

6. Make your adjustments as normal.

7. When you are ready to send the files back to Aperture, select **Export** from the file menu. This is where we will set up our export template.

8. For **Export To**, select **Hard Drive**.

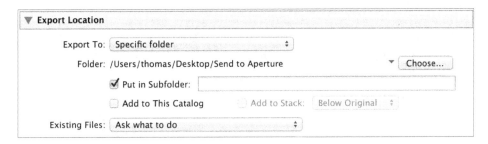

9. Under the export location, set it to the `Send to Aperture` folder you created earlier.

10. Scroll to the bottom and set any other option you need to. Set the file format to TIFF, to preserve the maximum integrity. Make sure resizing is turned off. Under **Post-Processing**, set **After Export** to **Open in Other Application....**

11. Use the **Choose...** button to set the `Send to Aperture` workflow we created earlier, as the application to open with.

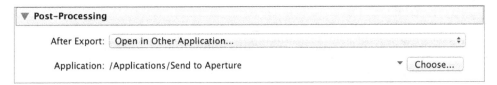

12. Save this template by clicking on the **Add** button, and call it `Send to Aperture`. From now on, all you have to do is select this from the **Export with preset** menu.

13. This will export the images, and then a pop-up dialog will appear asking where you want to import them to (this is that action running).

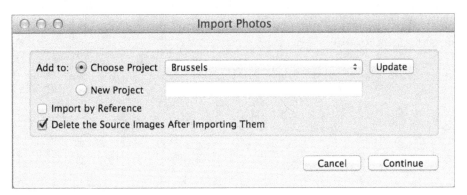

14. Select your destination project or make a new project. If you want to import the images by reference, tick that box, but this will leave the source images in the Send to Aperture folder. It is probably best not to do this. If you tick the **Delete images after importing** box, this will delete the images once they have been imported into Aperture, keeping your Send to Aperture folder nice and clean.

While that may have seemed like a complicated set of steps, once you have performed it, you only have two buttons to press between Aperture and Lightroom. To send to Aperture all you have to do is select the images in Aperture, and click on the **Send to Lightroom** application you created and saved to your dock. To send the edited images back, all you have to do is export with your **Send to Aperture** export preset. Everything else should happen automatically.

The only real disadvantage of using Catapult is that Catapult will stack the images with their original counterparts, but other than that this should work pretty much similarly.

Summary

In this chapter, we took an extensive look at ways to extend image processing in Aperture. We examined some recommended plugins that every Aperture user would benefit from having, as well as looked at some others that are also pretty useful. We then learned how to work with external editors, and looked at ways of working with the industry leader Photoshop, as well as some popular Photoshop alternatives. Finally, we looked at how to work with third-party RAW converters using the Catapult plugin, and we looked at a workflow for working with Adobe Photoshop Lightroom.

In the next chapter, we will move away from ways to process your images and we will look at how to work with metadata. Good use of metadata can make your life a lot easier, especially when you want to search for an image in the future. We will also see some real world uses of metadata, and why good metadata is an important part of professional photography.

6
Exporting and Outputting to the Web

In this chapter, we will discuss the best options for outputting your image for the web or to other online or offline digital services. Between the dominance of social networks such as Facebook and Twitter, and the fact that the web is the primary gateway for many professionals seeking to access new and existing clients, outputting your images in the correct fashion is a very important skill to have. How you prepare and output your images can actually have a big impact on how well your images will look when displayed on either your own website, a social network, or an image-sharing site such as Flickr or 500px.

In this chapter, we will cover the nuts and bolts of exporting your images. We will look at how to quickly export your images to your website, and how to take some time and do it in a way that preserves the best quality.

In this chapter, you will learn:

- Setting preview settings
- Exporting versions and setting up export presets
- Blogging from Aperture – the easy way
- Blogging from Aperture – the proper way
- How to share to Flickr and Facebook
- A better way to share your images with Flickr
- Using export plugins
- Tweeting directly from Aperture
- Sharing with Photo Stream
- Creating a Portfolio for your iPad

Setting preview settings

There are a couple of ways you can export your edited images out of Aperture.

- You can export them using the dedicated export function
- You can drag-and-drop images into another application
- Or you can access your images through the OS X media browser, which can be found in every open and save dialog box

We'll cover the dedicated export function in the next section *Exporting versions*, but first let's look at the other two options.

If you drag-and-drop an image out of Aperture, you will get a JPEG copy of your edited image. Aperture does this instantly, and you may be wondering just how it's able to do it so quickly. It actually uses the previews that Aperture creates when you import, and edits those preview images. You can control the quality of these exported preview images by going into Aperture's preferences. The same applies to the images accessed through OS X's system-wide media browser.

We briefly covered how to change the preview settings in the previous chapter, but to recap, this is what you have to do shown in the following:

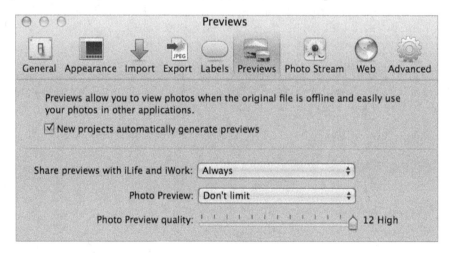

1. Go to the **Preferences** option in the **Aperture** menu.
2. Click on **Previews**.
3. Make sure **Share Previews with iLife and iWork** is set to **Always**.
4. If you want your images to be full size, set **Photo Preview** to **Don't limit**.
5. Set **Photo Preview quality** somewhere between 10 and 12. If you want it to be the best quality set it to 12.

Remember that the higher the quality settings you choose, the better your exported images will look, but this comes at the expense of disk space.

Any time you change the preview settings you will need to update your existing previews. Do this by selecting your images and right-clicking on an image, and then holding down the *option* key and selecting **Generate Previews**. Previews are stored in your Aperture library file, so if you notice that your library size is increasing after changing these settings, this may be the reason.

Using OS X media browser

In every open and save dialog box in OS X there is a special media browser that can be accessed by going to the bottom of the side bar. If you scroll down you will see a section for photos and for videos. If you look under the photos heading you will see a section for both iPhoto (if you have it installed) and Aperture. If you select the Aperture option you will see all the projects in your current Aperture library, as shown in the following screenshot. From here you can select any image.

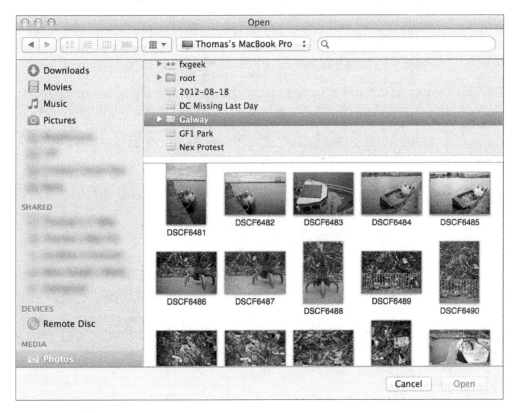

This is a great tool that is often forgotten about by many users. It is accessible from any application that uses a standard OS X open and save dialog box, and it makes it very easy to access your images without having to export them first. There are a few downsides though. You are limited to the size settings available in the previews preferences. You can't arbitrarily set your image dimensions and you can't include a watermark this way. However, the media browser option is always available, even when Aperture is not running, so if you are in a hurry this method can be very useful. It even works with offline images. For example, if you have stored your image files on an external hard drive, and the drive is not currently connected, you can still use the photos in your library using this method. This is because this technique uses the previews, and the previews are stored in the library file. So as long as your library file isn't on the external drive, you can still access your images through the media browser.

Exporting versions

The proper way to export images, the way that gives you the most control, is to export a version. You can do this by either right-clicking on an image and choosing **Export Versions** or by going to the **File** menu and choosing **File | Export | Versions**. The keyboard shortcut for this is *command + shift + E*. You can also export multiple images at once. To do this, select the images first and then choose the export function.

Choosing the export command brings up the somewhat complicated-looking export dialog sheet. Aperture's export function is actually pretty powerful. It might look daunting at first, but it is pretty flexible and once you get the hang of what it does, you will be surprised at just how much thought the engineers have put into it. Let's go through some of the options in more detail.

Export Preset:	JPEG – 50% of Original Size ⇕
Subfolder Format:	None ⇕
Custom Subfolder Name:	Enter folder text here
Name Format:	Current Version Name ⇕
Custom Name:	Enter name text here
File Name Example:	DSCF7290.jpg
	☐ Show alert when finished

New Folder   Cancel   Export Versions

1. **Export Preset:** This is where you set the format you want to export. There are a selection of presets already included that cover a variety of formats and sizes. You can select a preset that matches your needs, you can edit one of the existing presets, or you can create an entirely new one. We will take a detailed look at export presets in the next section *Setting export presets*.

2. **Subfolder Format:** This is another very powerful feature that is often overlooked. You can have Aperture automatically create subfolders depending on certain criteria contained in your image metadata. So, for example, you can have it create a subfolder based on the project the image is from, or the date it was created, and so on. There are a number of presets already set up for this. If you want to export your images and have them sorted by month, for example, choose **Image Year/Month** from the drop-down menu. This will put your images into folders for each different month of the year in which your selected images were captured in. This is also handy if you're exporting multiple versions of images and want to sort them while exporting. This is also highly customizable.

3. **Custom Subfolder Name:** If you have set **Custom** as your subfolder format, then this field allows you to enter the name for the folder.

4. **Name Format:** This is another template-driven setting. It decides how Aperture should name the files as it exports your images. Like the **Subfolder Format**, it is procedurally driven and can name your images based on metadata such as date and time of the image, or as a sequence with a custom name, and so on. Again, you can make your own templates for the name format.

5. **Custom Name:** If you have **Custom** set as your name format, this field will allow you to enter the name.

6. **Name Example:** This will give you an example of how the final exported filename will be like. Here you can get a quick overview of all your naming options and you can quickly see whether your files are going to be named the way you want them to be or not.

7. **Show alert when finished:** If you tick this option, Aperture will pop open a dialog box when you have finished exporting your images to let you know that the sequence is complete. If you have this ticked off, Aperture will export the images and then leave you alone.

Aperture exports images in the background, so once you set your options and start the process, you will be taken back to the main Aperture interface. You will see a little progress wheel in the bottom of the viewer window to indicate that Aperture is busy, and you can click on this if you want to see the progress of your export.

This brings up Aperture's activity window that allows you to see the progress of any background tasks currently running in Aperture. You can access the **Activity** window at any time by choosing **Window | Show Activity** or you can use the keyboard shortcut *shift + command + 0*.

You can also pause and cancel background tasks within the activity window from the **Pause Task** and **Cancel Task** button at the bottom left.

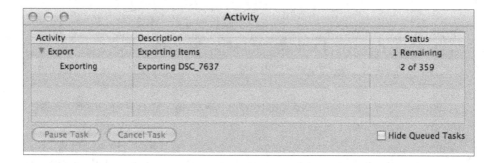

Because Aperture uses your computer's GPU to accelerate the export process, it exports images pretty fast when compared to other photo management tools such as iPhoto, so don't be surprised if you go to check on it and it has already completed the process.

Setting export presets

As we learned in the previous section, Aperture uses a number of templates to control the export process. You can easily edit existing templates or create your own new ones. The most important one to get to grips with is of course the main **Export Preset**. This controls the size and format of your exported images and allows you to set a watermark too. There are two ways to access the template editor for export presets.

- You can access it by exporting an image, and from the **Export Preset** pop-up menu you can choose **edit**. This will bring you to the export preset editor window.

- From the Aperture menu choose **Presets | Image Exports**.

Once you have opened the export presets window, you are greeted with a two-pane interface. The pane on the left contains a list of existing presets, and the pane on the right contains all the options for that preset.

- To edit an existing preset, select the preset from the column on the right and start editing the parameters.

- If you want to make a new preset, you must actually duplicate an existing one. To do this, select an existing preset that is similar to what you want to create, and click on the **+** button at the bottom-left side of the window.

In the right-hand side of the window are the parameters that you can edit. They are shown in the following screenshot and described in detail in the following:

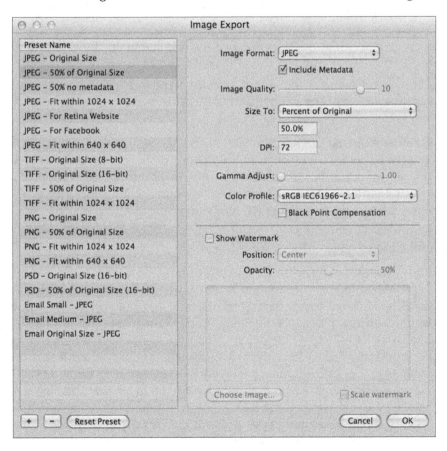

- **Image Format**: This can be any of the following file types: JPEG, PNG ,TIFF 8-bit , TIFF 16-bit, PSD 8-bit, or PSD 16-bit.

  If you are planning to use the image in another application, then you might want to consider using either of the uncompressed formats: TIFF or PSD; and to preserve best quality you should use 16-bit format. However, if you're passing an image on it will go straight to the output without further processing, such as desktop publishing, for example, then 8-bit is probably ok.

  If you're planning on sending an image to the web then JPEG file format is suitable, or if necessary, a PNG format. You should only use PNG for smaller images if you're going to use them on the web, as the PNG file size can be quite large for bigger images.

- **Include Metadata**: This checkbox tells Aperture whether or not to include the metadata with the image when you export it. Uncheck this box if you don't want your metadata exported with your image, but be aware that important information such as ownership and copyright will also be excluded.

- **Size To**: This section gives you options for setting the size of your image. You can set it to **Original Size**, which will preserve the original size of the image, or tell it to be a percentage of the original image by selecting **Percent of Original**, or finally you can tell it to fit within a certain size.

  There are options for the unit of measurement and DPI. If you're using centimeters or inches as your unit of measurement, you can set the DPI to control how the image is scaled.

- **Gamma Adjust** and **Color Profile**: These settings allow you to set a different gamma for exports as well as telling Aperture what color profile to embed. If you're exporting to the web, it is probably best to set the color profile to **sRGB**. If you're sending the image on to another editor for further work then you may want to use **AdobeRGB** or something similar.

  Alternatively you can set it to **Use Source Profile**, which will use the embedded profile of the original image.

- **Show Watermark**: The final checkbox option allows you to set a watermark to be embedded on your image. You can drag-and-drop an image into the drop zone to be used as a watermark, or you can click on the **Choose Image...** button and select the file manually. The image may be a TIFF, PSD, PNG, or JPEG file type. Ideally you should use an image with a transparent background. PNG or PSD files with a transparent background are good formats to use. (Ideally multiple layers in a layered PSD file should be merged into a single layer, but don't flatten the image as flattening it would lose the transparency information). The **Position** option tells Aperture where on your image you want to place it, and the **Opacity** slider controls how transparent the watermark will be.

Watermarks are resolution dependent. So, for example, if you have a 3000 x 2000 pixel original image and a 500 x 300 pixel watermark, it would appear in a certain size. However, if you use that same watermark for a larger or smaller original image, your watermark will appear smaller or larger (respectively) because it's still at the same resolution.

There is an option for scale, **Scale watermark**, which scales your watermark depending on the size of the image. But it's a bit confusing and there's no way to control it. It is better to design your watermark for the size you intend to use in your template beforehand.

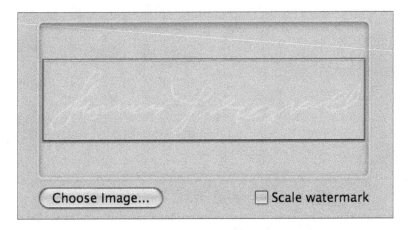

If you're using a watermark at the bottom corner of your image, be aware that Aperture places it right in the corner, so if you want to keep some space around the edge, you need to build that into your watermark file.

Once you're finished editing your presets, you can click on the **OK** button to exit out of the preset editor and save your changes.

Filename and folder templates

The templates for filenames and folders are very similar, and they too can be accessed by going to the Aperture menu and selecting **Presets | File Naming** or by selecting **Presets | Folder Naming**. As with the image export presets, you can also access the preset editor by choosing the edit option from the corresponding pop-up menu in the export dialog box.

As both of these templates are very similar, we will just take a look at the **File Naming** template, which is shown in the following screenshot. The same techniques also apply to the folder name editor.

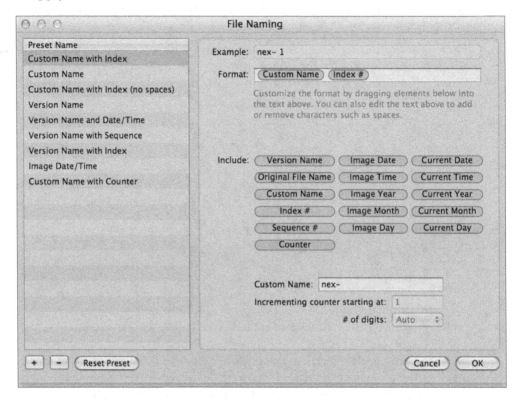

As with the image format editor, the interface for the **File Naming** editor contains a list of presets on the left and the parameters on the right. In the parameters section, you will see four main areas, which are as follows:

- **Example**: An example at the top, which shows an example of what the filename will look like
- **Format**: A field for entering options
- **Include**: A collection of procedural tags that you can use
- **Custom Name**: And finally, a field for a custom name, so you can set the default that appears in the open and save dialog

To edit a preset you simply drag the tags into the format field. Each tag contains a parameter that is replaced based on metadata or some other calculation at the time of export. So, for example, **Image Date** from the **Include** section will insert image date into the filename where you place the tag. You can also directly type into the format field so if you want to add additional characters you can, and also you might want to add delimiters between tags, such as a hyphen, underscore, or even just a space. Although if you are putting your images on the Web, you might not want to use a space as it complicates the URL of the image, and requires special characters to handle the space. If you want to set it up so that you can choose a custom name at the export stage, add a **Custom Name** tag into the **Format** field.

Once you've set your options you will see an example of what they will look like at the top of the window. To save your presets, click on **OK** to exit the dialog box.

Blogging from Aperture – the easy way

If you have a website for your photography, you probably also have a blog too. Posting images to a blog is probably one of the most common things that many modern photographers do. But how do you get your images from Aperture into whatever service you are using, be it Tumblr, WordPress, or Blogger. As with many things, there is a quick way, and a better way. Let's look at the quick way first.

Before you export your images, it is always a good idea to add some metadata first. Even if you only add a title to your image, that will be something. If you want to change the filename that will be used when using this method, then you need to change the **Version Name** field, which can be found by clicking on the info panel. The procedure is shown in the following screenshot. We will cover adding metadata in more detail in the next chapter.

Title:	
Version Name:	Pinocchio
Headline:	
Caption:	Pinocchio statue outside a shop in Vienna
Keywords:	
Copyright Notice:	
Date:	16/02/2013 22:22:34 GMT
Pixel Size:	4288 × 2848 (12.2 MP)
File Size:	18.97 MB
Project Path:	Vienna Day 2
Badges:	

Once you have your images ready to export, go to your blogging software and write your blog as normal. At the time of choosing an image you can do one of two things. If you are using the latest versions of WordPress or Tumblr, both allow you to drag-and-drop images into their respective **Add Media** options, and you can literally drag-and-drop images from Aperture directly onto their windows.

However, because both the Aperture window is fairly large, and the WordPress window can be large, unless you're working on a big screen or a computer with multiple monitors, this may become a little unwieldy. You can of course shrink the Aperture window first.

An easier way is to use the media browser in the open and save dialog box. Here in the following are some instructions for adding an image to a WordPress blog:

1. In your blog editor click on the **Add Media** button.
2. Click on the **Upload Files** option if it is not already selected.
3. Click on the button that says **Upload media from your computer**.
4. In the open and save dialog box, scroll down to the bottom of the side bar and select **Photos**.
5. Select your Aperture library and find the project you were working on.
6. Select the image you want to upload.
7. Click on **OK**.

Your images will now be uploaded to WordPress.

Remember that images are uploaded using this method, otherwise the drag-and-drop method will be output using the preview settings, so make sure you have set those properly beforehand.

What is wrong with this method

There are three main issues with using this method when blogging images from Aperture:

1. The first is that it uploads full-size images. Even if you don't have your preview size set to full resolution, it will still likely be way bigger than you need.

2. Secondly, you can't embed a watermark with this method, and you may wish to include a watermark of some kind when uploading images to be displayed on the Web.

3. Thirdly, even if you are okay with the first two problems, WordPress (and other services) aren't using as good a quality-scaling algorithm when scaling images as a desktop program does, and when they do, the images may appear softer than if you scale them yourself.

So with these three issues is that, as you can see, it is best to take a little more time and do it the proper way. So what is the proper way?

Blogging from Aperture – the proper way

To best present your images on your website, you should export your images from Aperture in the settings that best suit your website. To start with, you should determine what size you want your images to be and have Aperture scale those images to the correct size. This can either be the size you want them to appear on your webpage, or if you want to have them opening large in a light box on your site, then enter the size you want them to appear there. Also, remember that if you are making your website HiDPI or Retina Display compliant, so that they are compatible with Apple's retina displays on their newer laptops or the iPad and iPhone, you need to double the size of your images (although with retina resolution images you may be able to get away with a higher compression).

Here are the steps to take for maximizing quality when blogging from Aperture:

1. Start by creating an image export template for your blog. Set the size as discussed before to the size best suited for your site. Your format should be JPEG, and you want to set the quality somewhere between 7 and 11. Remember that the higher the quality setting, the bigger your file will be. You don't want to be filling your webpage with lots of huge files, so keep it as low as you can while still maintaining the best quality. Personally, I use a setting of 8. You may also want to add a watermark. Prepare your image in Photoshop or one of the alternatives mentioned previously, and add that to your preset.

 This may sound obvious, but test out your presets a few times with different types of images so that you are happy with the settings before you go to use them on your website.

2. Select your images in Aperture and export them to a folder on your hard drive by choosing **File | Export | Versions**.

3. From your WordPress (or Tumblr and so on) interface, choose the option to upload images, and locate the folder on your hard drive that you exported from, and select the images to upload.

The advantages of this method over the quick way are that the images are optimized for the size of your website and are not too big, and they can contain a watermark.

 When I export images from Aperture to use on my blog, I use Dropbox, and export images to a special folder inside of my Dropbox folder. The reason I do this is that I have my main Aperture library on my workstation in my office, but I often write my blog posts from my laptop. This way I can easily access the exported files without having to do any messy file transfers. Plus, because they are on Dropbox, I also have a handy backup. Some people might be concerned about security or privacy concerns when using Dropbox, but as we're talking about images you intend to blog, you're going to be posting them to the Web anyway, so it really shouldn't be a big concern. If you are sending confidential images to a client, you might want to consider the privacy implications of using a Cloud-based service such as Dropbox.

Export plugins

Just as with image editing, the export architecture in Aperture supports a robust plugin ecosystem. There are lots of plugins available that allow you to send your images directly to various online services as well as other destinations, for example, social networking sites such as Twitter.

Apple has a list of popular export plugins on its website. You can find it at the following URL:
`http://www.apple.com/aperture/resources/plugins.html#export`.

This doesn't list all of them, however, and is actually pretty backdated. Other popular plugins include some from developers such as Blue Crowbar, which can be found at `http://bluecrowbar.com`.

And Connected Flow (which provides a Flickr export plugin for Aperture) can be found at `http://connectedflow.com/flickrexport/aperture/`.

There are too many plugins available to look at all of them, but in the following we will examine a couple of popular ones that are valuable to have.

TwitExport

This software can be found at Blue Crowbar; it is available at `http://bluecrowbar.com/twitexport/`. The price charged is $3.99 at present.

This is a very useful plugin that allows you to tweet an image directly from Aperture. Once you have it installed, you just choose **Export | TwitExport**, and a window will pop open with options to enter your message to go along with your image. The plug-in uses your export presets as templates for how to format your image, so it can include watermarks if you have TwitExport set up. It connects to two different image services (including the popular TwitPic) to handle the image hosting. It's simple and does exactly what you want it to.

BorderFX

This software can be found at iBorderFX; it is available at the following link http://www.iborderfx.com/borderfx. It's free/shareware.

BorderFX is a handy plug-in that allows you to add borders and frames to your images when exporting it from Aperture. It has a comprehensive set of options and you can do some interesting things with it. It has a powerful watermark feature that, unlike Aperture's built-in watermarks, allows you to create a watermark using just text. Even without the actual border functions, you can use it for that alone. It also lets you add sharpening to your image at export time, making up for one of Aperture's most bemoaned missing features, export sharpening. You can also create presets using the various border styles that you come up with yourself, so you don't have to enter settings each time you export.

500-Wide

This software can be found at Blue Crowbar; it is available at the following link http://bluecrowbar.com/500-wide/. The price charged is €2.99 at present.

The photo sharing site 500px has become very popular recently and this plug in from Blue Crowbar will let you export directly to your 500px account. It allows you to add keywords or use your existing Aperture keywords and to set the 500px category for your image.

iStockPhoto Uploader

This software can be found at iStockPhoto; it is available at the following link

```
http://www.istockphoto.com/aperture
```

The software is free.

This is a useful plug-in if you are a contributing photographer for the popular stock photography site. With this plug in you can set the necessary metadata and upload straight to iStockPhoto directly from Aperture.

PhotoShelter Uploader

This software can be found at PhotoShelter; it is available at the following link:

```
https://support.photoshelter.com/entries/21625348-Apple-Aperture-
Plug-in
```

You are not charged for this software. If you use the popular image archival and hosting service, PhotoShelter, this plugin allows you to export directly from Aperture to the service.

Exporting to Facebook and Flickr

If you are a social media user, you may use one or both of these two popular networks. Aperture has built-in sharing options for both of these services. You can share your images directly to Flickr and Facebook from the share menu in the Aperture toolbar. This allows you to create a new album (or "Photo Set", to use Flickr's terminology) and set the size of the images you want to export, as well as set some privacy options.

However, there are a few issues with using these sharing functions within Aperture. For a start, the options are very limited. You only have limited control over how images are scaled, and you cannot add a watermark. On Facebook, you can't send media to a Facebook page. But if you're using Facebook as a photographer, you are probably using a Facebook page rather than your personal profile. On Flickr, you can't add images to groups during the upload process, and you can't add additional metadata other than what you already have included in the file.

Managing Facebook

If you are just posting images to Facebook for personal use then the existing sharing options are probably fine. If you are publishing to a Facebook page then it would be better if you export your images to your hard drive first and follow the same guidelines as outlined earlier for blogging your images.

To share a set of images on Facebook, using the built-in functionality, you must first connect to your Facebook account. You do this by going to menu and then choosing **Aperture | Preferences** and then selecting the **Web** tab.

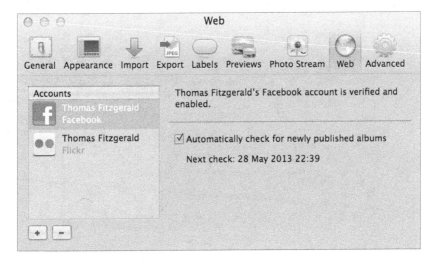

Here you can add Facebook and Flickr accounts. To add a Facebook account click on the plus (**+**) button at the bottom of the preferences tab. This will pop out a sheet from the window's title bar, asking which kind of account you want. Select **Facebook**, and enter your details.

This will then connect Aperture to your Facebook account, and your existing Facebook albums will be downloaded to Aperture. A Facebook entry will now appear in the Aperture sidebar under the web section.

If you click on this, you will get a grid of your existing Facebook albums. You can go into any of these albums and see the photos that have already been uploaded to Facebook. At the bottom of the window, you will see a Facebook drop-down menu. Clicking on this will give you some options, including the option to visit the album page on Facebook.

To share some photos, select your photos in Aperture and from the **Share** button on the toolbar, select Facebook.

This will pop up a sheet with the Facebook sharing options as shown in the earlier screenshot. In this pop-up you can choose to upload to a new or existing album, to name that album if you are creating a new one, and to set the privacy options. Click on **OK** and your images will be uploaded to Facebook.

Facebook usage terms

You should be aware of Facebook's terms of service before posting images to Facebook. In essence, by agreeing to the terms and conditions, you're granting Facebook unlimited rights to use your images. This doesn't mean you're signing ownership of your images over to Facebook, it just means that you grant them the right to display and use the images however they want. There are arguments that this is a legal requirement that a service such as Facebook needs to have to be able to operate and avoid being sued. But some people think that this goes too far. There are a lot of different opinions on the practical implications of using Facebook, and much of this opinion is quite polarized. One could write a whole book on this issue alone. You should be aware of this issue and you may want to take some time to educate yourself on the pros and cons before sharing your photos on Facebook.

Facebook's full terms and conditions can be seen at the following link:

`https://www.facebook.com/legal/terms`

Managing Flickr

The Flickr sharing options within Aperture are similar to the Facebook ones, and it works in a similar fashion. To add an account in Flickr, follow the same procedure as you did for Facebook, but choose Flickr instead and carry out the following instructions.

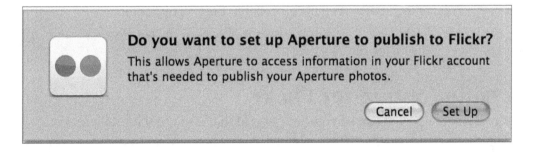

When you add your account, you will get a Flickr entry in the sidebar, and clicking on this will show you your existing Flickr photo sets. To share with Flickr, as with Facebook, select a series of photos and, from the pop-up share menu, choose **Flickr**.

The sharing sheet will pop open and you will have the following options:

- **Set**: This is the photo set you want to add into. It can be an existing one or a new photo set.

- **Set Name**: If you are creating a new photo set this field lets you name the set.

- **Photos Viewable By**: This is where you set, the privacy options.

- **Photo Size**: This is where you set the size you want to upload. You have three options.

  - **Full Size**: This option uploads your images at the full resolution of the image file.

  - **Optimized**: This option uploads your images at a smaller resolution of the image file. This is probably the best option here.

  - **Web**: This option uploads your images at the smallest resolution of the image file.

A better option for Flickr

There is a better way to export your images and that is to use the excellent FlickrExport plug-in from Connected Flow.

FlickrExport

This software can be found at Connected Flow; and the downloadable file is available at the following link:

`http://connectedflow.com/flickrexport/aperture/index.php`

You are charged £14.

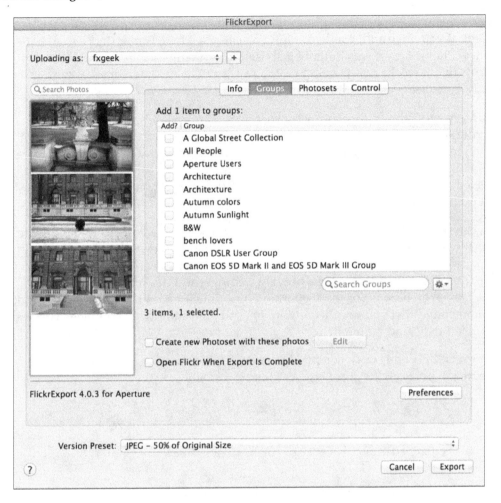

FlickrExport is a great plug-in that supports most of Flickr's options. You can set the exact size you want to upload, and you can embed a watermark because it uses Aperture's export preset templates for resizing. You can also add your images directly to Flickr groups from within the plug-in interface. You have complete control over how it handles Aperture metadata, including how it handles keywords for Aperture tags. You can also edit the description and title for each image you are uploading, apart from the Aperture name and caption information. This can be useful if you need to add additional information to the Flickr image that you don't want in the standard caption info. For example, you might want to include background info on the shot, or HTML links to a blog post about the shoot. All this is possible by using the FlickrExport plug-in.

Sharing with Photo Stream

Photo Stream is Apple's own photo sharing and syncing service that is a part of iCloud. If you have an iCloud account, you can use Photo Stream as part of that service. Photo Stream was initially just used for syncing images between devices, and for that it works really well. But you can also use it to share images with friends, family, or colleagues.

Setup is pretty straightforward because it uses your system's iCloud settings. In order to activate Photo Stream within Aperture, just click on the Photo Stream button in the sidebar, and then click on the button that says **Turn On Photo Stream**. This will open a status sheet that says **enabling Photo Stream**, and once that are finished, Photo Stream will connect to iCloud and start downloading any images that is already in the Cloud.

You can set Aperture to automatically add any new images to your Photo Stream so that whenever you import photos from your camera they will be automatically uploaded to iCloud, and get shared with your other devices. Note that this only uploads a JPG version (using the preview settings) and doesn't actually upload RAW files. However, because of the 1000-photo-at-a-time limit on Photo Stream it is not recommended that you use this option. Instead, you should share images you want to upload to iCloud manually.

To turn on or off this option, go to **Aperture | Preferences**, and from the **Photo Stream** tab uncheck the checkbox **Automatic upload**.

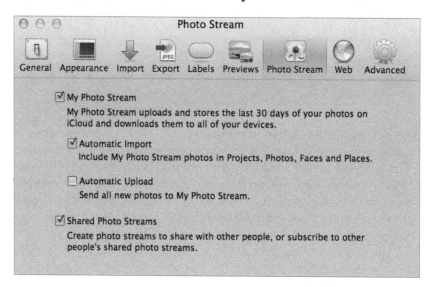

To add images to your photo stream you can do one of two things. You can drag them onto the Photo Stream section of the Aperture sidebar, or you can select your images and choose **Photo Stream** from the sharing pop-up on the Aperture toolbar. This will bring up the Photo Stream share sheet, which is shown in the following screenshot:

From here you can choose an existing Photo Stream (that is, your main stream or one you have created earlier) or a new Photo Stream. If you choose to create a new one, you will get additional options which will let you name the Photo Stream, enter the e-mail address of people you want to share it with, and whether or not you want the stream accessible via a public website hosted on icloud.com.

This last option is handy if you need to quickly share some images with a client, for example. It's fast and easier than sending a whole lot of photos in an e-mail.

Creating a quick iPad Portfolio with Photo Stream

If you are an iPad owner, one of the things you may use it for is showing off your photos. It is a very handy tool to have to show prospective clients (or helpless family and friends!). One of the things many photographers like to do is keep their Portfolio on their iPad. One way to do this is to create a `Portfolio` album in Aperture and then sync it through iTunes to your iPad. But what if your Aperture library is not on the computer you sync your iPad with? What if you don't sync your iPad to your computer at all? This is where Photo Stream comes into play.

You can simply create a new Portfolio Photo Stream and this will sync via iCloud to your iPad (and any other devices that you have). Here's what to do in the following steps:

1. Select the photos you want to include in your Portfolio. It is probably easier if you create a root-level album for your Portfolio within your library first.

2. With your photos selected, press the share button on the Aperture toolbar, and choose **Photo Stream**.

3. Choose the option to create a new Photo Stream.

4. Name it `Portfolio` or something similar. You don't need to enter an e-mail address at this stage, but you can always just e-mail it to yourself.

5. If you want you can enable the option to share on the Web via iCloud but you don't need to for this process.

6. Click on **OK** and your Photos will start uploading to iCloud.

7. On your iPad go to your photos app. Then go to the **Photo Stream** section. You will now see a Portfolio thumbnail in there. This will be your new Portfolio.

8. You can add new images to your Portfolio any time by choosing **Share | Photo Stream** again from the Aperture toolbar, and selecting your Portfolio as the destination.

9. If you want to remove items from your Portfolio, click on the Photo Stream icon on the Aperture sidebar, and select your Portfolio. You can now delete individual images from within the Portfolio Photo Stream.

Summary

In this chapter we took a detailed look at exporting your images from Aperture. We discussed the preview settings and how Aperture uses the previews function to allow you to control both drag-and-drop images from Aperture, and how they appear in OS X's system-wide media browser. You learned a quick way to blog your images, and a better way. We looked at export plug-ins and how to share your images on Facebook and Flickr as well as how to tweet your photos directly from Aperture.

In the next chapter we will take a detailed look at metadata, and why it is important. You will also learn different methods.

7
Making Metadata Work for You

Having good metadata is an incredibly important aspect of digital photography that is often overlooked by most amateurs (and even some professionals). Proper keywords and entry of other descriptive information, not only ensures that you can later find your photos, but also that if you send your images to a client or a service, they can properly catalogue and sort your files. Aperture has powerful metadata tools and is leading in its ability to edit and manage metadata. In this chapter we will look at a few examples of why this information is important. We will also look at the ways of quickly and efficiently entering this data.

In this chapter you will learn:

- Why good metadata is important
- How to use the Info tab
- How to set up list views
- Viewing all EXIF data
- Creating metadata templates
- Different ways of entering keywords
- How to enter captions and titles quickly
- Using TextExpander to speed up data entry
- Batch replace metadata
- Adding custom metadata
- Searching and smart albums

Why good metadata is important

There are lots of reasons as to why you should become efficient and diligent when it comes to properly cataloguing your files. If your images have proper keywords and captions, it becomes a lot easier to find them at a later date, when you have a large library. Finding files in your library is only one example of why metadata is important and keywords and captions are just some of the information that you can embed.

For example, if you use a stock photography service to sell your photography, having proper metadata will be a requirement of that service, and it aids you in selling your images. Because most search engines can't understand visual data, you need to be as descriptive as possible. Many services also have rules about what other information you need to add. Even if you are just posting images to your own website, it is important that you have copyright information and contact details embedded in your images. If you shoot sports or press photography, your publishing service may also have requirements for what metadata you need to embed.

In practical terms, even if you are just an amateur, publishing photos on your blog then having good metadata can have real world advantages. For example, if you are using WordPress, it will access the caption and title information, and embed it in your images on the web. When I started making sure that proper metadata was embedded in my images when I posted them, I found that my website traffic increased by a measurable amount. Having good keywords when posting to a service such as Flickr will increase the ability to find your images by quite a bit.

Aperture's Info tab

To view and edit your metadata, you need to switch to the **Info** tab in the main inspector as shown in the following screenshot. This is where most of your metadata wrangling will occur. At first glance this might look like an innocuous section of the Aperture interface, but there is a surprising amount of information that can be displayed and edited here.

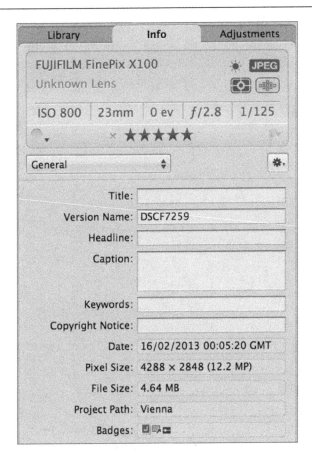

At the top of the **Info** tab you will see the camera display panel. This panel shows details about the camera you used to take the shot, exposure information, the white balance, exposure mode, and file format you used to take the shot. There is also a useful function here that lets you see the focus point that you used when you took the shot. If you hover over the focus point button, you will see an overlay of which focus point was selected when you took the shot. You can also toggle this button to display the focus point without having to hover over it. This can be useful if you're trying to troubleshoot some out of focus issues.

Beneath the camera info panel are the flagging, rating, and label options. Here you can see if your images have a star rating, a color label, or if they have the flag turned on or off. You can also change any of these options by clicking on them. Beneath this are two drop-down menus. The first selects which set of metadata is displayed. This is controlled using presets, and we will look at that in the next section of this chapter. On the right-hand side of the panel is a cog menu, with some functions that you can use to manipulate your metadata.

In the main part of the window, the metadata itself is displayed. What gets displayed here depends on the list preset you have selected in the drop-down menu. Aperture defaults to a preset called **General**. It displays the following metadata fields:

- **Title:**
- **Version Name:**
- **Headline:**
- **Caption:**
- **Keywords:**
- **Copyright Notice:**
- **Date:**
- **Pixel Size:**
- **File Size:**
- **Project Path:**
- **Badges:**

Most of these are fairly self-explanatory, but let us look at a few of these in detail:

- **Version Name::** This is the file name that Aperture uses for the image. Version names must be unique.

- **Title:** and **Headline::** These fields might seem like the same thing, but they can be used differently by various photo services. If you are a press photographer, for example, your service may require you to use the **Headline:** field. Other services, such as iStockPhoto, for example, require the title of the image to be put in the title field.

- **Caption::** This is where you give your image a long description. While titles and headlines should be one sentence short descriptions, the caption can be as long as you want. The more descriptive the caption, the easier it will be to find your photo in an online service.

- **Date::** This displays the date and time that your image was taken at, as opposed to the import date. You can actually display the import date by customizing the view.

- **Badges::** Badges in Aperture are icons that denote that various changes have been made to an image, and whether or not an image is referenced. They are normally shown on the bottom of an image, but they can also be seen in the info panel, as shown in the following screenshot:

For a complete list of what each badge icon means, there is a whole section in the Aperture manual, which you can view online by going to the address:

`http://tinyurl.com/18qfskq`

Metadata View templates

The information displayed in the general view is only a small fraction of the information that can be part of an image's metadata and which can be viewed in Aperture. You could set it up so that you can see all the information, but this would quickly become a huge headache for entering the data, as you would have to scroll through a long list to find the fields that you want to use. Instead, Aperture uses a number of metadata view templates to control what is displayed in the info panel.

Aperture comes with a number of these view presets included by default. Let us take a look at a couple of these in detail, and when they might be useful.

Name Only

This lets you see and enter just the **Version Name:** as shown in the following screenshot. This preset is useful if you want to go through your images and change just the version name, as it hides all other distractions.

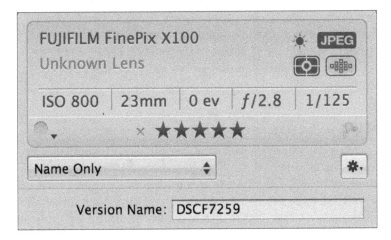

Caption Only

Like the name only option, this displays just the caption field. However, if you only want to see the caption, there is another caption entry preset that is even better.

Large Caption

This preset gives you just a caption field, but it is made larger to give you lots of room for entering text as shown in the following screenshot:

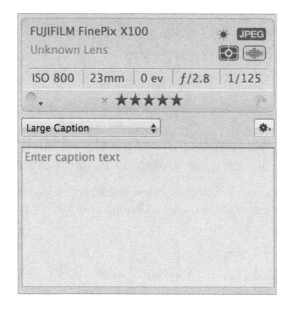

EXIF Info

This preset shows a selection of the embedded camera information that is part of the standard camera specification. It doesn't, however, show all the available data in the EXIF specification. Aperture can display this information, but you can manually configure a template to do so.

IPTC Core

This shows a standard set of metadata that follows the **International Press Telecommunications Council (IPTC)** specification. IPTC developed a set of standard information to be included with images. It is traditionally used by photographers who are photojournalists or press photographers. If you work for a wire service they may require that many of these fields be filled before submitting your photographs.

For more information on IPTC visit their website at:
`http://www.iptc.org/site/Home/`

Creating your own templates

You can create your own metadata view templates quite easily, as well as edit existing ones. These should not be confused with metadata presets which we covered in *Chapter 1*, *Advanced Importing and Organizing*, which contain presets for commonly used metadata.

To edit the list templates, go to the info panel, and from the drop-down menu choose **edit**. This will bring up the **Metadata Views** editor as shown in the following screenshot:

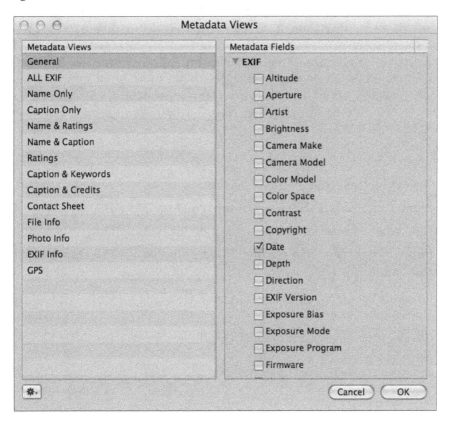

On the left-hand side of the window you will see a list of currently available templates, and on the right-hand side you will see an extensive list of all the metadata you can display. While you can display any of the entries here, not all of this information is editable. Some of it, such as camera info, can only be viewed.

To create a new preset, choose **New View** from the drop-down cog menu at the bottom of the preset window. If you want, you can also choose to duplicate an existing view. Name your new template, then go through the list of metadata on the left-hand side and check any checkboxes for the metadata fields that you want to be displayed when you select that template. When you finish the task, click on **OK** to exit the dialog.

Create a preset to view all EXIF information

As mentioned earlier, the EXIF view preset that comes with Aperture doesn't actually show all available EXIF information. It might be a good idea to create a new preset that shows this data. It can be useful to have, if you are having trying to troubleshoot issues with your camera or even just trying to figure out something technical about your photography to aid in improving your work. For example, if you have shot a JPEG and you can't remember what sharpening settings your camera used, but the existing template doesn't show this information, you can still access it as it is embedded in some camera's metadata. To do this you need to enable it in a Metadata View template.

To create a template for viewing all EXIF information, complete the following steps:

1. Select any photo and go to the info panel.
2. From the **Metadata Views** drop-down menu select **edit**.
3. When the views editor is open, select the **EXIF** info preset.
4. From the cog menu at the bottom of the window, choose **Duplicate view**.
5. Rename your template EXIF All or something similar.
6. From the list of metadata scroll to the **EXIF** section (it should be already at the top of the view).
7. Check everything under the **EXIF** heading.
8. Click on **OK** to exit the editor and save your preset.

The page will look like the following screenshot:

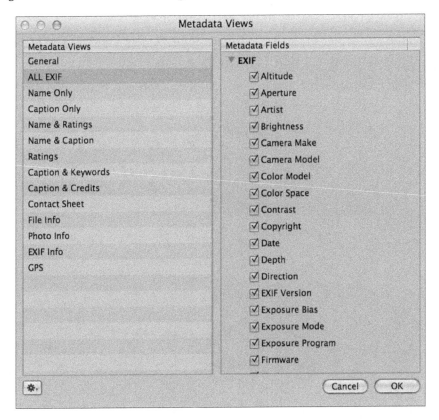

You now have a view that will let you see every piece of information that your camera has embedded in the image file when you took the photo.

 To reorder the list, all you need to do is click-and-drag a field name in the info panel, and you can drag it up or down in the list.

Creating metadata templates

Now that you have an understanding of how to control what information gets displayed with Metadata View templates, you can move on to setting up templates for the actual data itself. We covered this briefly in *Chapter 1, Advanced Importing and Organizing*, and it is the same technique used to enter information in the import dialog. However, there are a couple of extra tricks that you can do in the info panel that are worth knowing. First let us take a quick look at how to create presets.

There are two ways you can get to the metadata presets editor:

1. In the Aperture menu go to **Presets | Metadata**.

2. On the info panel, click on the cog drop-down menu and choose **Manage Presets**.

Either of these methods will open the preset editor as shown in the following screenshot:

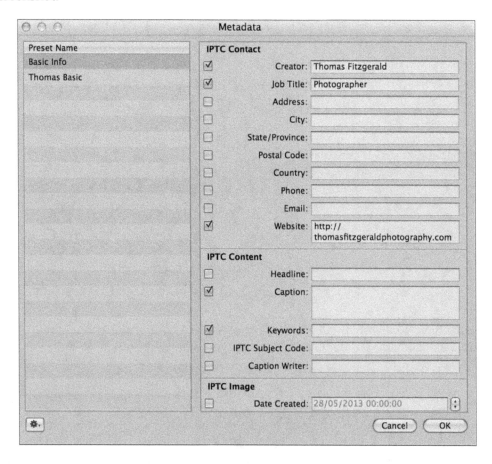

Once you are in the editor, you can create as many presets as you want in addition to any presets that you may have previously created, to be applied on import. For example, if you work for different wire services, you can create presets that contain the relevant information for both.

There is another quick way to create a metadata preset in Aperture that doesn't involve going to the editor first. If you have a photo selected, and you have entered some metadata into it, you may want this to be the basis of a template for future use. To save your currently entered metadata information as a template, complete the following steps:

1. Make sure you are in the info panel and you have already entered the metadata that you want to save.

2. From the cog drop-down menu choose **New Preset from version**.

3. This will open the preset editor with a new preset created, and any fields that you have changed will be filled in with a tick box beside them.

4. Give the new preset a name.

5. If you want you can edit it further, now that you are in the preset editor. You may want to uncheck some tick boxes if you had entered information for a particular entry, but don't want that to be part of the metadata template.

6. Click on **OK** to exit the template editor and save your preset.

Different ways of entering keywords

Keywords are an invaluable tool when it comes to finding your images at a later date. Entering keywords can sometimes seem like a laborious task, but there are ways to make it easier. In fact there are lots of different methods of entering keywords in Aperture. There are at least five different ways, so it would seem that the programmers really want you to use keywords! You can enter keywords using the following methods:

- On import in the import dialog
- From the info panel
- From the Keyword HUD
- From the keyword control bar
- With the Lift and Stamp Tool

We have covered entering keywords on import in the first chapter.

Entering keywords from the Info tab

Entering keywords on the info panel is pretty straightforward. Select an image, and make sure you are on a view that has the keywords field displayed as shown in the following screenshot. You can now start entering keywords and can separate individual keywords with a comma. It is important to note that keywords are case sensitive. For example, if you enter boat it will be treated as a separate keyword from Boat. You can also enter whole phrases as a keyword.

One very important limitation of entering keywords in the info panel is that you can only enter keywords on one image at a time. If you want to apply keywords to multiple images at once then you need to use some other method.

Using the keyword HUD

The keyword HUD contains every keyword that has ever been entered into your Aperture's library at any time on any image. It also comes with a list of defaults. To get to the keyword HUD from the menu go to **Window | Keywords HUD** or press the keyboard shortcut *shift + H*. The page will look like the following screenshot:

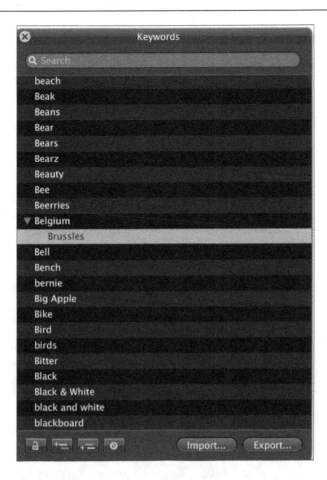

At the top of the keywords HUD is a search field. Here you can search for existing keywords and they will appear in the list below. You can of course just scroll through the list and find the keywords manually. If you find a keyword you want to use, you can drag it onto an image. If you have multiple images selected and you drag it onto them, it will be applied to all the images.

If the keyword you are searching for doesn't currently exist, you can create it here. At the bottom of the window, to the right-hand side of the lock button is the new keyword button. Pressing this will create a new blank keyword. Type your keyword and press *return*. You can now drag this onto your selected image or images.

You can also use the keyword HUD to manage existing keywords. For example, you can correct spelling mistakes, fix capitalization errors, and so on. If you change a keyword and it becomes the same as another keyword (which can happen when you fix capitalization errors), you have the option to merge keywords. This will update any images with that keyword applied.

Hierarchal keywords

Aperture supports a useful feature called hierarchal keywords. Basically, you can create a hierarchy of keywords. For example, say you create a keyword heading called `Travel`, you can then create sub keywords for different cities. So you could have a sub keyword for `New York` and another for `Paris`. Because these are sub keywords of the `Travel` keyword, if you apply `Paris` to an image, for example, and you then search for `Travel`, it will still find the image keyworded with `Paris`.

You can create a sub keyword in the keyword HUD by selecting a keyword you want as the parent, and then pressing the **Add Subordinate Keyword** (highlighted in the following screenshot) on the bottom of the keyword HUD.

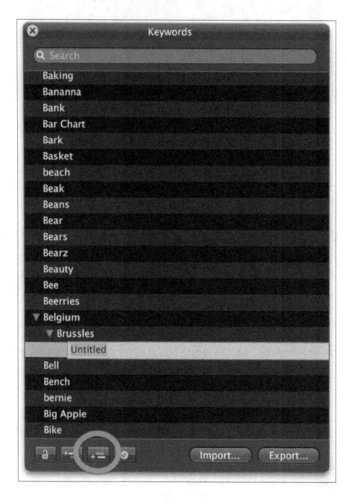

The Keyword Control Bar

The keyword control bar is probably the fastest way to enter keywords for multiple images, because it gives you a set of buttons that you can press with just a single click of the mouse. You also have a keyword entry field, which allows you to enter multiple, comma separated keywords, but unlike the info panel, you can apply keywords to multiple images at once.

To access the Keyword Control Bar from the window menu choose **Show Keyword Controls**. The control bar will appear beneath the main viewer window. On the bar you will see a set of buttons for various keywords, a keyword entry field, and a drop-down menu. From this drop-down menu you can select from a set of preset button sets, or you can select the **edit** option to create your own. The keyword control bar will look like the following screenshot:

To apply a keyword from one of the buttons to the image, simply select an image or multiple images, and press the button for your chosen keyword; it's that simple. To remove the keyword, hold down the option key, and press the button. You can also use keyboard shortcuts to apply the first eight keywords from the set. Select some images and then hold down the **option** key and press the numbers *1* to *8* for the corresponding buttons. If you hover over the buttons you will see the corresponding shortcuts.

To enter keywords manually here, simply enter them into the keyword entry field. Note that as you type, any existing keywords that match what you are typing will appear and you can select these without having to finish typing the complete word, as shown in the following screenshot:

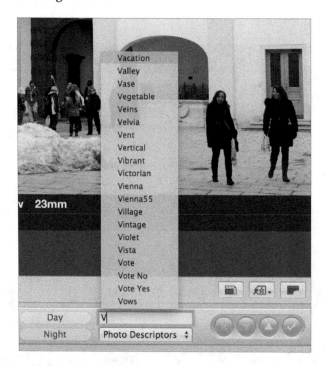

Lift and Stamp keywords

You can lift and stamp keywords (and other metadata) between images just as you can with adjustments. When you use the lift tool, you need to make sure you are not stamping adjustments too. Use the lift tool on an image and then select any information, adjustments, and so on from the lift, and stamp HUD that you don't want stamped onto other images, and delete them as shown in the following screenshot. Then you can stamp the other images with just the keywords that you have lifted.

Entering captions and titles quickly

If you want to caption a lot of images in one go, the process can be quite monotonous. It doesn't have to be though, because Aperture has a neat little trick that can speed up the procedure substantially. To use this method, you have to enter one piece of information at a time. So if you need to enter captions and titles, enter all the titles first and then enter all the captions. To explain how this works, we are going to focus on adding captions by way of example, but this will work for titles, version names, or any other text-based field. You should have your images narrowed down to just the ones you want to caption before you start. Here's how this works:

1. Switch to the info panel, and from the views drop-down menu choose **Large Caption**.

2. Select the image you want to start with, and in the caption field enter whatever text you want as a caption.

3. When you are finished doing this, before you click anywhere else, press *command* + right arrow button.

4. This will move to the next image; the caption field will become active and the text insertion point in the field will be all ready for you to type.

5. Continue this process for the rest of your images.

The dialog looks like the following screenshot:

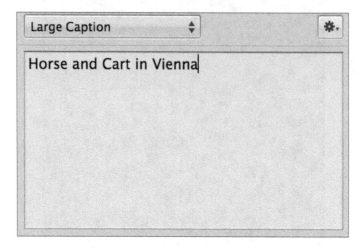

With this technique you can speed through your selected images and quickly caption them all. You can use tricks such as copying and pasting here too, and because everything can be done with the keyboard you don't have to be constantly moving back and forward between the mouse and the keyboard.

This method will work with any editable field that can be displayed in the info panel. So long as you don't click out of it, pressing *command* + left or right arrow button will take you to the next or previous image with the selected field still highlighted.

Using TextExpander to speed up data entry

If you find that, when you are entering metadata, you are entering the same information over and over again, then you may find that an auto completion tool may speed up data entry. While OS X has a rudimentary autocomplete function built-in, using a third-party one will offer greater flexibility. In this section we are going to look at using the excellent TextExpander from Smile Software as the tool of choice.

TextExpander

The link for downloading the Text-Expander tool of Smile Software is
`http://smilesoftware.com/TextExpander/`. The TextExpander tool
looks like the following screenshot:

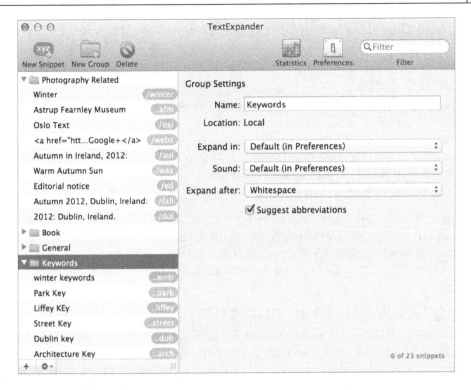

TextExpander allows you to replace text as you type. You define a preset set of shortcuts that can be any short strings of text. Every time you type one of these shortcut strings, TextExpander will replace that shortcut with whatever text you have pre-defined. These text replacements are called **snippets**. TextExpander has some useful functions, such as the ability to group snippets into sets, and the ability to sync your settings between computers with iCloud. You can even enter styled text and HTML as a snippet. We give two examples of how this tool can be useful for the Aperture user.

Entering long strings of text for captions

If you regularly enter the same text over and over in the caption information, then you can replace that with a shortcut. For example, say you are shooting a shoot in New York city and you want to begin your captions with:

```
New York City, November 2013
```

Simply set this up as a snippet and give it a shortcut. You should use something that you wouldn't type by accident, so adding non-alphanumeric characters can help. For example, for this text you could use something like /ny.

Now every time you type /ny it will be replaced by `New York City, November 2013`.

Keyword sets

If you regularly use keywords you may find yourself using the same keywords over and over for the same topics. If you are using image services or stock photography sites, they may require you to be as descriptive as possible, and so you need to enter linked topics when you are entering keywords. For example, if you are taking shots of birds, you would obviously want the keyword `Birds`, but may also want to use connected terms such as `Avian`, `Flight`, `Nature`, `Wings`, `Sky`, and so on.

Because Aperture can accept comma-delimited text in the keyword field, you simply set up a string of keywords separated by commas as a text snippet and give it a shortcut. For this example, something such as `..bird` might work. Here we are using the double period at the start so that we won't activate the replacement by accident.

Using OS X's built-in autocomplete

As mentioned earlier, you can use the OS X's autocomplete functionality if you don't want to buy a third party tool such as TextExpander. To set up snippets using the operating system tools, start by opening your computer's system preferences (by choosing it from the Apple menu, or from the Dock) and do the following:

1. Click on the **Language & Text** button.
2. Click on the **Text** tab.
3. Make sure the **Use symbol and text substitution** checkbox is checked.
4. At the bottom of this column, click the **+** button.
5. In the first entry, enter the shortcut you want to use.
6. In the second entry, enter the text you want to replace.

The **Language & Text** page will look like the following screenshot:

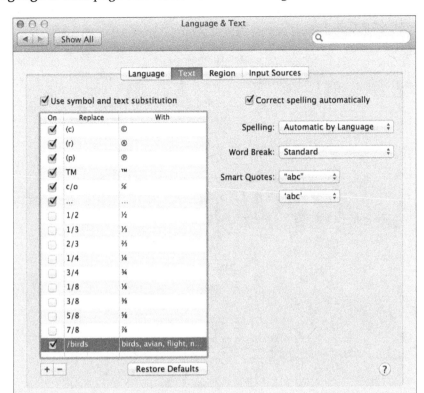

Batch changing metadata

If you need to update the metadata on a lot of images at once, then you will be pleased to find that Aperture has a very useful batch change tool. With this tool, you can apply the same data to lots of images at once. You can also use it to append new information to existing metadata.

To bring up the batch change dialog from the Window menu choose **Batch Change**. You can also get to it from the cog drop-down menu on the info panel as shown in the following screenshot:

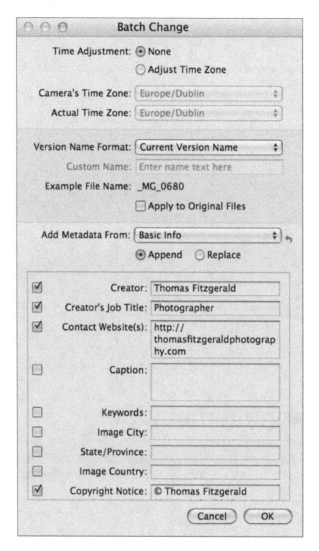

The **Batch Change** dialog is broken into three main sections. The first controls updating or changing the image's time stamp. This is similar to the controls on the import dialog that we covered in *Chapter 1, Advanced Importing and Organizing*.

The second section allows you to batch change the file's version name. This uses the same procedural techniques and templates as the file naming options for exporting. In fact it uses the same templates that we covered in the previous chapter.

The third section allows you to append or replace any of the metadata fields. It is based on the metadata preset templates, the same ones used at import, and you can either replace from one of the templates or use it as a starting point. If you choose to replace, it will replace the entire corresponding field. If you choose the option to append, it will add the information to the end of any existing metadata.

Adding custom metadata

Aperture has another powerful metadata tool in its arsenal, and that is the ability to create custom metadata. With this function you can create your own metadata fields and they can be used for anything you choose.

There are a couple of ways to add a custom field. From the info panel, click on the cog menu and choose **Manage custom fields**. This will bring up the custom field editor. Here you can create new custom fields as shown in the following screenshot. The problem is, once you create them, they won't actually show up in the Metadata View until you add them to a view preset.

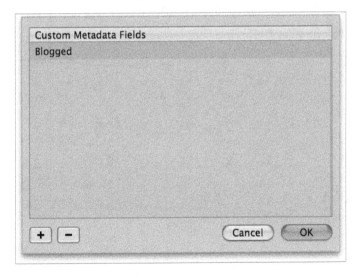

The better way to get to the editor is to open the view editor by choosing **Edit** from the view preset drop-down on the info panel. When the Metadata View editor is open you can choose **Manage custom fields** from the cog menu at the bottom of the window. You can now enter as many fields as you want. Once you are finished doing it, click on **OK** to close the custom fields sheet. Now all you have to do is add the newly created fields to a view preset. You will find the custom fields at the bottom of the metadata list. Check the checkboxes to add them to your Metadata View preset.

There is one limitation to custom fields and that is they can only be alphanumeric. While this isn't a big limitation, be aware that you can't have checkboxes or lists as options.

Some examples of when to use custom metadata

If you are wondering why or when you might need to use custom metadata, here are a few examples as some inspiration:

- If you shoot film and scan that film into Aperture, you can create a custom metadata field for the kind of film that the images were taken on.
- If you submit your images to a stock photography service, you can create custom fields to track the status of your submissions. Possible options could include: submitted, approved, and rejected.
- If you regularly blog your images, you can add a custom field to enter the web address of the blog entry that an image is posted to.

The page will look like the following screenshot:

Title:	
Version Name:	DSCF7309
Headline:	
Caption:	Horse and Cart in Vienna
Keywords:	
Copyright Notice:	
Date:	16/02/2013 22:12:00 GMT
Pixel Size:	4288 × 2848 (12.2 MP)
File Size:	19.00 MB
Project Path:	Vienna Day 2
Badges:	
Blogged:	no
Stock Submission:	
Blog Address:	Submitted

Searching and smart folders

Once you have all your metadata information entered into Aperture, you need to be able to use it. This is where Aperture's powerful search tools come in. There are two types of search in Aperture: you can search by entering search terms in the search window, or you can create smart albums, which will constantly update based on the search terms that you give it.

The search HUD

To see the search field at the top of the main window, you need to be in grid view mode. Switch to multiple mode or grid mode by pressing the *v* key on your keyboard to cycle through the viewer modes. When you are in grid view, you will see a search field at the top of the window as shown in the following screenshot. Beside that is a button that brings up the search window.

You can enter text directly into the search field and Aperture will search any text-based metadata for the text string that you type. To get more options, click on the **search HUD** button beside the search field. You can also get to this by pressing *command + F*. The page will look like the following screenshot:

Most of the options here are pretty self-explanatory, but there are a few hidden options that you should be aware of. At the upper-right corner of the window is a drop-down menu labeled **Add Rule**. This allows you to add additional search parameters based on any metadata that Aperture knows about. This can be useful if you have added custom metadata, for example, but it can also be used to search for camera attributes, such as lens used, focal length, aperture, and so on.

Here is an example. Say you wanted to search the Aperture Library for every shot taken with a Canon 5D Mark II with a 50 mm lens. The following is what you would do:

1. Go to the root level of your library.
2. Press *command* + *F* to bring up the search HUD.
3. From the **Add Rule** dropdown choose **EXIF**.
4. A new line will appear on the search HUD.
5. Tick the **EXIF** check box on the new line.
6. Set the first field to **Camera Model**.
7. In the second and third field (the text entry one) enter Mark II.
8. Add another rule and choose **EXIF** again.
9. Select **Focal length** as the key, and enter 50 as the amount.

The result will look like the following screenshot:

Aperture should now be showing you all the images in your library that were taken with the 5D Mark II and shot with a 50 mm lens. As you can see, the search functionality can be quite powerful as you can combine many different search parameters into quite complex searches. If you want, you can save this search as a smart album by clicking on the **New Smart Album** button at the bottom of the search window as seen in the preceding screenshot.

Smart albums

Smart Albums are basically saved searches, but they are "live"; this means that they are constantly being updated. If you had saved the search from the preceding example, and you added new shots to your library that matched the search parameters, they would automatically appear in the smart album.

To create a Smart Album there are two different approaches. You can search your library as we did earlier, and then save that search, or you can create a new smart album by choosing the **New** button on the Aperture toolbar, and selecting **Smart Album**. This will create a new Smart Album in the sidebar with a search HUD attached that you can then enter search terms for the album as shown in the following screenshot:

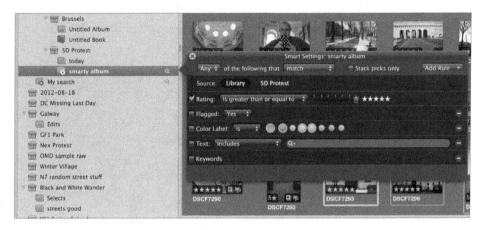

When you create a Smart Album you will see that there is a little magnifying glass beside it in the side bar. If you want to edit the search parameters of the smart album, just click on this little icon, and it will bring the search HUD back up.

Summary

In this chapter we took an extensive look at adding and managing metadata in Aperture. We looked at the many ways to manage your data and how you can view your data. We talked about why metadata is important and we looked at some ways to streamline the entry of this valuable information.

Now that you have learned how to import, process and catalogue your image, and how to output them to the web, in the next and final chapter, we will add the final piece of the puzzle and look at printing your images. We will cover both printing to a connected printer, ways to use the book module to layout your prints, as well as ordering prints from an online service.

8

Getting Better Prints from Aperture

If you regularly print photos from Aperture to your own printer, you probably already know what a minefield of options it can be. Printing can be something of an art form in and of itself, and within Aperture, there are numerous settings that can help you get the best quality prints. This chapter will help you navigate the sea of jargon surrounding the art of printing from Aperture, and teach you how to get better prints.

In this chapter you will learn about the following:

- Calibrating your display
- Onscreen proofing
- Understanding the print dialog
- Print sharpening
- Creating print presets
- Printing to PDF
- Creating digital contact sheets
- Using the book tool for advanced print layouts
- Ordering prints using Apple's service
- Ordering prints via a third-party service

Calibrating your display

If you are serious about printing from Aperture, or from any software, the single most important thing you can do to enhance the quality of your prints is to invest in a hardware display calibrator. It used to be the case that calibration hardware cost hundreds of dollars, but today a good display calibrator can be bought for around $100. While you don't strictly need a display calibrator to print, there are numerous advantages of having one. To understand why it's important, let's take a very quick look at the underlying technology, ColorSync, and how it affects your printing.

The problem with imaging technology is that all color is not created equal. Every device you own sees, displays, or outputs color slightly differently. You have undoubtedly had the problem where you tried to print something, but the colors on the print looked completely different from the colors on the screen. To get around this problem Apple developed a technology called ColorSync. You have probably heard the term before as it's been around for quite some time. What ColorSync does sounds quite simple, but it still causes confusion to many first-time users.

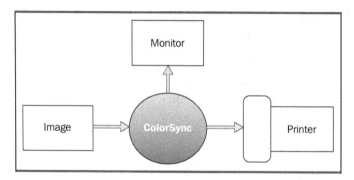

In essence, the ColorSync engine has profiles for your display, your printer, and so on. It knows the differences between each and is able to translate your colors so that when you print something on your printer, which has a different color space from your monitor, you still get reasonably accurate colors. ColorSync knows how your monitor displays color, it knows how your printer should display color, so it translates between the two. When you print, it applies the necessary modification to your image's colors, so what you print matches what you see on screen. For this to work properly, ColorSync needs a correct profile for your printer and your monitor. How your printer outputs color depends on the inks used, the paper used, and the settings chosen. Most manufacturers of high-end printers will supply a color profile for their printer. You can usually get profiles for various paper stocks too, so if you use a popular printer with popular quality paper, you should be able to get a color profile that will match the output side of the equation. You also need a profile for your monitor.

While many monitors come with color profiles, the problem is that the colors on all monitors drift over time. What might be accurate in the factory will soon be inaccurate after some time using it. There are ways to calibrate your display with just software, and OS X comes with a built-in basic method of calibrating your screen by eye, but such methods are not particularly accurate. In order to properly generate a profile for your display, you really need a hardware calibration tool.

Choosing a display calibrator

There are two main manufacturers of calibration hardware. The first is X-Rite, which make popular brands such as the ColorMunki and the i1Pro. The other is Datacolor, which make the popular Spyder hardware. Most of these products perform similar functions, but vary on additional functions and accuracy. You should buy the best you can afford. It is an investment that will make a huge difference if you plan to do a lot of printing.

 X-Rite can be found at `http://x-rite.com`.

For more information on Datacolor's tools visit `http://spyder.datacolor.com`.

Calibrating your screen

Calibrating your screen serves two purposes. First, it will change the way your screen displays colors, so that it is more accurate to how color is perceived in the real world. The first time you do this you might be in for a bit of a shock. Most people are used to seeing whites on their monitors with a yellow or blue tint, but when calibrated, one, first instinct is often that they look kind of purple. This is just because you are not used to it. It's actually more accurate, and once you've used a calibrated display for a while, you will find it hard to go back to a non-calibrated one.

The second function of calibrating your display is to create a color profile. This is the information ColorSync needs so that it knows how your monitor displays color.

Once it knows your monitors color profile, and it knows how your printer prints color, it can accurately print.

The calibration process itself depends on the software that comes with your display, but they generally follow the same procedure. The first step is to measure the ambient light in the room. Then, you place the calibration sensor on your screen, and the software will cycle through a range of colors. As each color is displayed, the sensor measures it and stores the information as part of what is called a look-up table. Once this process is complete and the software finishes its operations, it creates a standard ICC color profile that ColorSync will use.

Calibrate often

Another important consideration of having your screen calibrated is that you need to calibrate it often. Color on displays drifts over time, so it is very important that you regularly update your profile. How often you need to do it depends on the amount of printing you do, and how critical your color output needs are. Most manufacturers recommend that you calibrate your display every two weeks, and this is good advice. You should certainly do it at least once a month.

The limitations of calibration

While calibrating your display will get you reasonably accurate color, there are limitations. Because monitors create color based on direct light, and printed colors are based on reflective light from pigments on a page the range of colors each method can display is different. Also, each monitor and each printer has limits as to what colors they can display or print. With ColorSync and a calibrated monitor you will be close, but because of the differences between the gamut of displays and that of printed images, there will always be some differences in color reproduction.

Onscreen Proofing

One of the tools Aperture has to help overcome this difference between monitors and printed images is called **Onscreen Proofing**. What **Onscreen Proofing** does is simulate what the printed image will look like, by using your printers color profile. It will give you a better idea of what the printed image will look like, and it should show up any issues with colors being out of gamut on the printed page.

To use **Onscreen Proofing**, you first have to set up your proofing profile. From the **View** menu, navigate to **Proofing Profile**, and select the profile that matches the output you are going to be using.

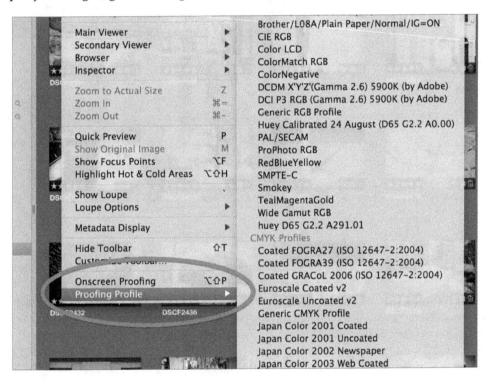

When you select a **Proofing Profile** for the first time, Aperture will turn on, **Onscreen Proofing**. You may notice slight changes in the colors of your image. To turn it off again, from the menu, navigate to **View | Onscreen Proofing** or use the keyboard shortcut *option + shift + P*.

Onscreen Proofing isn't perfect, but it will give you an indication if any colors are out of range, and it should show up any colors that will be significantly different on the printer you are planning on printing from.

The print dialog

When you print to a connected printer in Aperture, you will first go to the Aperture print dialog. This is a complex window that shows lots of options and can be a bit daunting at times. There are also some things that don't quite work the way you would expect. We will look at these in the following section, and you will learn to avoid some common problems.

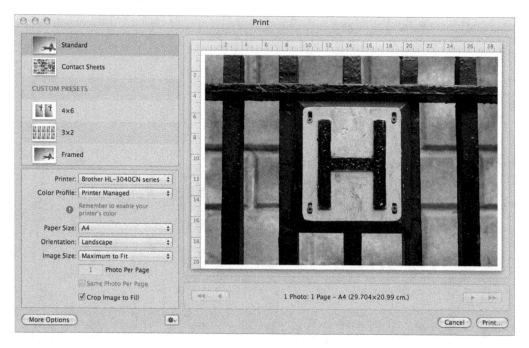

The print dialog is made up of three main panes. On the right, you have the main preview area. This is where you can see what your printed page will look like, with a visual representation of your pages' margins, any text that will be printed with the image, and if you have more than one image on the page, you can see the layout here too. When you have your page set up with margins or multiple images in Aperture, the image you see is actually a frame based on the size you set in the controls (more on this in a minute). You can control the size of this frame and the scale of the image separately, and you can do this directly in the preview pane, because the preview is active.

To see the controls, hover over the image in the preview pane of the print dialog. As you move your mouse over the area, you will see a dotted outline of the invisible grid that is making up the page layout. If you click on the image, you will get a pop-up control that allows you to adjust the size of the image, but the frame will stay the same. You can also pan the image around inside the frame.

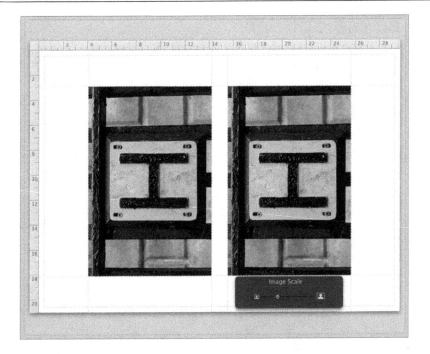

On the top-left you have a set of presets. These allow you to store common print layouts. You have options for contact sheets, multiple images on one page, and of course standard layouts, such as full page and framed. You can duplicate and tweak any of these presets to create your own versions.

On the bottom-left you have the controls. This is where you can select things, such as the printer you want to print to, the page size, the orientation, and the color profile. You can also control how many images are on the page, and whether you want the same image to be printed multiple times (if you have more than one image on the page), or if you want multiple images printed. This is actually just a basic mode though. There are a lot more settings, but they are hidden by default.

Set your color profile

If you have calibrated your display and you are ready to print, make sure you set your printer's color profile in the color profile pop-up menu. If you just leave it to printer managed, the ColorSync engine won't properly match colors.

Show all the options

To see all the options Aperture has for printing, click on the **More Options** button at the bottom of the print dialog.

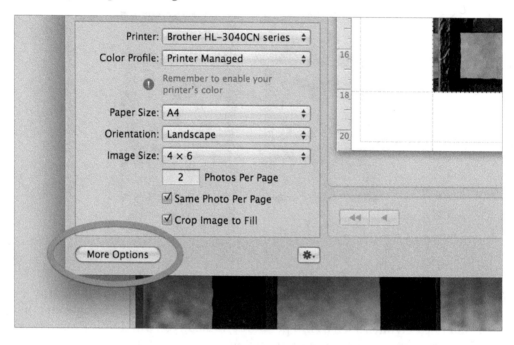

The **More Options** button will bring up a lot of important controls. There are a great deal of options here (no wonder they hide them by default) that add a lot more control to the printing process. They are as follows:

- **Layout**: This section contains controls for page orientation and image size as per the basic controls, and it adds options for the **rows and columns** controls, as well as **row and column spacing**.

- **Margins**: This lets you control the margins on the printed page.

- **Rendering**: This adds resolution to the basic color profile option. We will cover this in more detail in a moment.

- **Image Adjustments**: This allows you to control the brightness and contrast of your image, prior to printing. If you're having issues with prints matching your expectations, you can use these controls to make some adjustments and tweak the output. There is also an option here for print sharpening. We will cover print sharpening in detail a little later in this chapter.

- **Image Options**: This section allows you to set a border for your image, determine the rotation, or even add a watermark to your print.

- **Metadata and Page Options**: These controls allow you to print metadata, such as captions, image titles, and so on with your image. This is useful for contact sheets and printing proofs. You can also use this section to add page numbers and crop marks.

Most of these are self-explanatory, but let's take a look at a few of them in detail.

Print resolution

This setting allows you to control the size and resolution that your image is rendered at, before it is sent to the printer. This causes some confusion for a lot of people, because it is not the same as your printer's print resolution. They are two different things. Your printer's DPI, which might be a value such as 5600, is the number of droplets of ink the printer uses to create an image. As the printer uses a halftone pattern to create shades of color, the resolution needs to be much higher than the image resolution. It might take hundreds of drops to create a single pixel of your actual image, and the finer the pattern of ink droplets, the more accurate the color and the print will be. By comparison, the resolution setting here controls the number of pixels per inch that is rendered by Aperture.

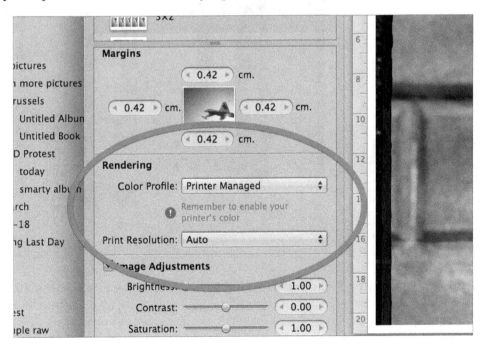

By default Aperture sets this value to **Auto**. If you have a high-end printer, then this setting is not recommended because it often prints at too low a resolution, depending on your printer. With a high-end printer, you should set it to a setting of 300 dpi or higher. In reality, you may need to do test prints to find the best settings for your printer.

Print sharpening

Print sharpening applies sharpening to your image at the time of printing, and is not the same as the sharpening controls in the adjustment brick. The reason that Aperture (and most photography software) has a print sharpening option is because most printers actually soften the image slightly due to the halftone method of printing. By sharpening an output you can compensate for this. This is a control you need to be careful with however, as overdoing it can make your prints look over sharpened.

You can get a preview of the print sharpening by clicking on the **loupe** button (the small loupe icon beside the **Sharpen** controls), which will bring up a loupe over the image. You can move this around and inspect various parts of your image at 1:1, and see a preview of your sharpening. The settings you need to set will depend on your printer, but a good starting point based on experience is the following:

Amount: 1.00

Radius: 0.50

You may need to make some test prints and experiment with these settings to get your setup just right for your printer.

Creating print presets

As with many things in Aperture, you can save your set of settings in the print dialog as a preset. There are already presets for some common page sizes and print types, included as default, such as the **Contact Sheet** preset or the **Standard** preset. However, if you are regularly printing to different sizes or to different setups, you may want to create a preset for your printer and paper combinations so that you are not changing settings every time you want to print.

Creating print presets is actually a little counterintuitive because you should create the preset first, and then change the settings, rather than changing the settings and then saving it as a preset. You also must start with one of the existing templates, as you can't create a new one from scratch.

To create a new print preset, perform the following steps:

1. Select an existing preset that is close to what you want to use.

2. From the cog pop-up menu select **Duplicate Preset**.

3. You will now have a new preset named after the original preset, but with the word **copy** appended to the end of the name. The name will be highlighted and is editable, so you can rename it now.

4. Make the changes that you need to make to the preset.

5. From the cog pop-up menu, click on **Save Preset**.

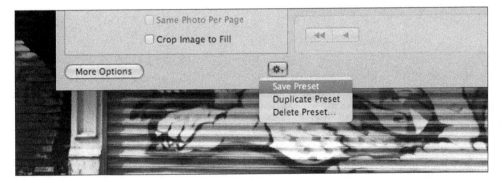

Issues to be aware of when creating print presets

There are a couple of odd things about the behavior of the print dialog and the way it handles presets that you should be aware of. As I mentioned earlier, you should duplicate an existing preset before making changes to it to create your own. However, if you start with an existing template and then make changes, you can still duplicate this preset, but the original will keep the changed settings too. However, these settings will be lost once the print dialog is closed. You can see which presets that haven't been saved in the preset section of the print dialog because they have a little dot beside them to let you know that they are unsaved.

When you attempt to close the print dialog, you will get an error letting you know that you have unsaved presets, and Aperture will offer to save them for you. This is where you can run into trouble. If you have made changes to an existing template and then decided to create a new template by duplicating it, and you had forgotten to save the new template when you closed the print dialog, then you are left with the following two options: you can either write over the one that you changed before you duplicated it, or you can lose the new one that you have just created.

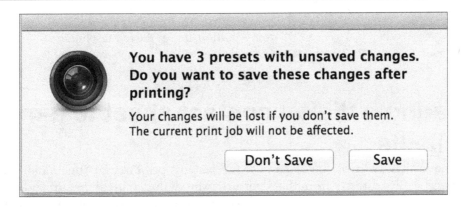

It's an unfortunate bit of programming because you can't go through the presets and decide which one to keep, and you also can't cancel closing the print dialog. However, if you are aware of this in advance and get into the habit of duplicating the base template before you start making changes, then you should avoid this somewhat unpleasant scenario.

Printing and saving to PDF

Like all applications on OS X, Aperture can create a PDF file directly from the print dialog box. This can be useful in several ways, from sending proofs to a client with metadata and notes printed below the image, to creating digital contact sheets, or for sending multiple image layouts to another computer to be printed.

It may not be immediately obvious where these controls are, however, as they are not located directly in the Aperture print dialog box. This is because Aperture's print process is actually two staged, and when you click on print in the print dialog, you will then be taken to your printer's default print window where you can then select the PDF options. The following is a breakdown of how to get to this option in detail:

1. Select your image or images.
2. From the menu choose **File | Print** or press *command + P*.
3. This will bring up the **Aperture Print** dialog. Set up your print in whatever way you choose.
4. Click on the **Print** button.
5. This will bring you to the standard system print dialog.
6. From the PDF pop-up menu, select **Save as PDF**.

When you save a PDF from Aperture, it uses the full resolution of your image and it is not compressed, so the file may be quite large.

Creating a digital contact sheet to e-mail to clients

As we have already learned, you can use the systems print to PDF functionality to save the PDF files directly from the Aperture print dialog, with all layout and other settings you may have set intact. One good use for this is for sending contact sheets to a client. In the past these were traditionally printed, and while that is still often the case, it is a common request now to have contact sheets delivered to a client via e-mail. The following steps will show you how to do this in Aperture:

1. Select the images you want to send to your client in Aperture, and make sure any metadata you might want to include has been entered.

2. From the **File** menu select **Print**.

3. This brings up the print dialog box. From the list of presets, select **Contact Sheet**.

4. If it is not already showing, select the **More Options** panel.

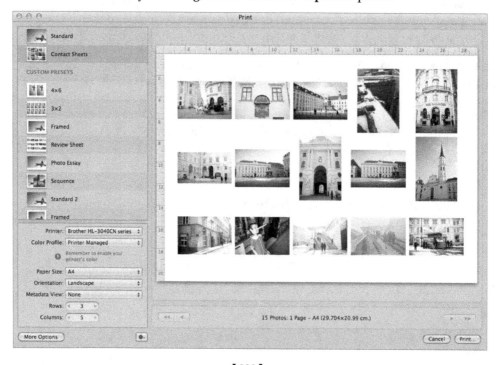

5. Adjust the number of rows and columns till your contact sheet looks the way you want it to.

6. If you want to print metadata under the images, go to the metadata section of the options pane.

7. From the **Metadata View** pop-up menu, select one of the views that you want to use. Aperture comes with a handy **Contact Sheet** view already predefined, which includes the version name, caption, and exposure information.

8. When you are satisfied, click on the **Print** button.

9. This will bring you to the standard print dialog.

10. From the pop-up PDF menu, select **Mail PDF** (if you don't want to e-mail the contact sheet, you can actually just choose **Save PDF**).

11. This will create a PDF of your contact sheet, and launch your e-mail client with a new message and the PDF attached.

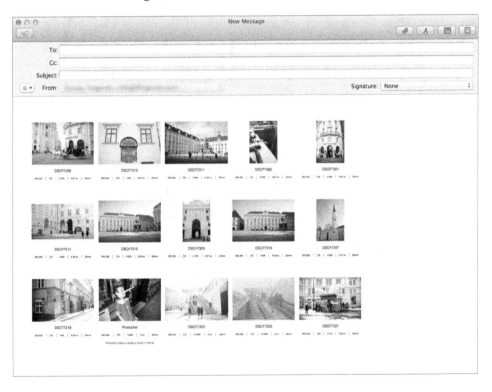

The Mail PDF workflow creates a low-resolution file that is ideal for e-mailing. If you want to send a full resolution contact sheet to someone, choose **Save PDF** instead of **Mail PDF**.

Printing to a JPEG file

Sometimes you or your clients may prefer a JPEG file to a PDF. Aperture used to include a very useful print workflow plugin (the ones that show up in the PDF menu of the print dialog) for saving a PDF file as a JPEG file. This functionality seems to have disappeared in more recent versions. Luckily, it is easy enough to add this feature back with a little trip to Automator. The following is what you need to do:

1. Launch Automator.
2. Select **Print Plugin** as the option, when asked to create a new window.

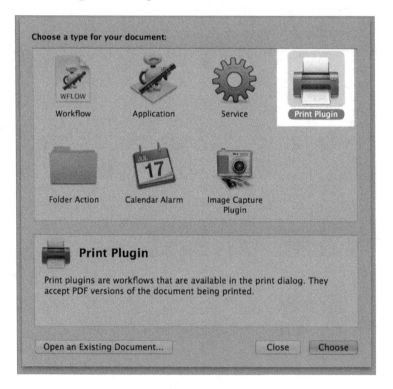

3. From the **Library** panel, select **Photos**.
4. Scroll through the list of actions and find **Change type of images**.
5. Add this to your workflow.

6. From the **Library** panel, select **Files & Folders**.

7. Search for **Move Finder Items**.

8. Add this to your workflow.

9. On the **Move Finder Items** workflow, click on the **Options** button.

10. From the options that are revealed, select **Show this action when the workflow runs** (this will let you select the folder at the time of running the action).

11. Save your workflow by navigating to **File | Save**, and give it a name, for example, `Print to Jpeg`.

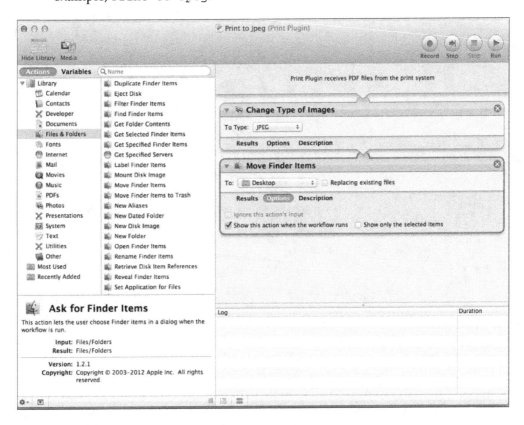

Now, when you go to save a PDF, you should find a new option in your PDF menu with the workflow you just created. If you select this when you print, your layout will now be saved as a JPEG file instead of a PDF file.

Using the book tool for elaborate print layouts

While the print dialog in Aperture contains lots of options for creating layouts for your prints, there are limitations as to what it can do. You have little control over adding text, and using multiple images on the page is limited and rigid. If you want to do something more creative, you don't actually have to leave the software to do it. That is because Aperture actually contains a pretty sophisticated page layout module. This powerful tool is hiding under the guise of the book layout module.

You are probably already familiar with Aperture's book module, as it is one of the key features of the software. Within Aperture, you have the ability to order printed photo books directly from Apple. To do this, the software contains a dedicated module for creating and laying out books. You can choose from a number of templates and add your images to the book. You can then upload this to Apple's servers and order a physical printed book. The process is fairly straightforward and you may have played around with this feature already. What is less commonly known is that you can actually use the book module's layout functionality to create your own custom layouts, and print them yourself.

To start using this function you need to first set up a custom theme. The following is what you need to do:

1. Start by selecting the image or images you will want to use in your print layout.

2. From the new menu on the Aperture toolbar, select **Book**.

3. The new book sheet will open. From the **Book Type** pop-up menu, select **Custom**.

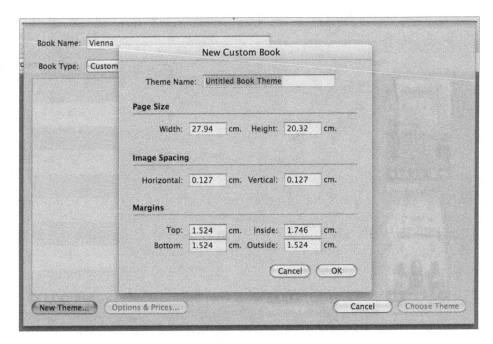

4. Here you will find a list of any custom themes that you may have already created. If this is your first time using this functionality, the list will be blank.

5. Click on the **New Theme** button at the bottom of the list.

6. This will bring up the **New Custom Book** dialog. Enter the settings that match the size of the page you are going to print. Give your new template a name.

7. Click on **OK** to exit the dialog.

8. You can now select your newly created template in the list. Give your new book a name, and click on the **Choose Theme** button.

9. You will now get a new empty book in the size that you have specified.

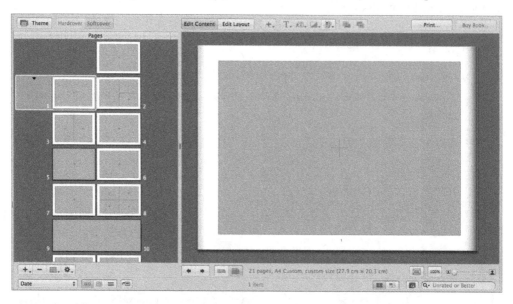

You will now have a new empty book that you can fill with images, or you can use a single page to create a nice print. The existing layouts may suit your needs initially, but if using the premade templates were all that you could do here, this wouldn't be very useful for laying out prints. Luckily, you can customize the individual layouts to suit your needs. Perform the following steps to customize a page layout:

1. Start by selecting a layout that is closest to how you want your final layout to look. You can do this by either using one of the pages of the book that is already set up and deleting the rest of the pages, or by using the **Page Layout** pop-up menu and selecting a layout.

2. To use the **Page Layout** pop-up menu, select a page in the **Pages** pane and click on the little arrow that appears beside the selected page. From here you can select one of the premade layouts.

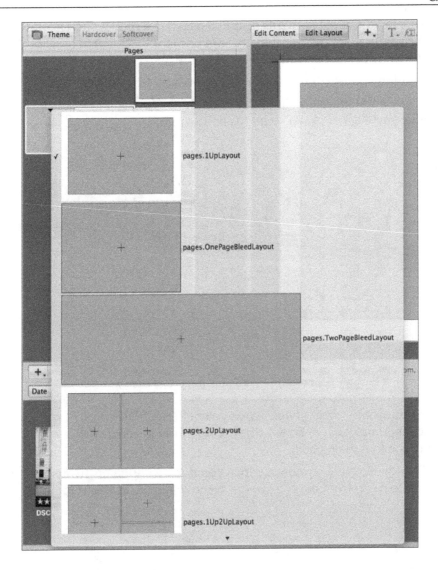

3. Once you have the layout that best suits your needs as a starting point, you can drop your image or images into the layout.

4. On the top of the book preview pane, click on the button that says **Edit Layout**. You can now use the page layout tools.

5. If you want to resize an image frame, click on it and drag the handles to make it whatever size you want. To reposition the image within the frame, either click back over to the **Edit Content** mode, or simply double-click on the frame.

6. To add additional elements from the page, click on the plus (**+**) button over the layout area, and select the type of element you want to use. For the purposes of this demonstration, select a textbox.

7. Position your textbox and enter some text.

8. To style the text, select it, and click on the **T** button on the toolbar. This will give you a list of preset styles to choose from.

9. If you would rather style the text yourself, right-click on *control* + click on the text and navigate to **Font | Show Fonts** from the contextual menu to bring up the font dialog box.

10. To hide the page numbers (which you don't want if you are just printing a single page) from the cog pop-up menu, navigate to **Page Numbers | Off**.

Once you are happy with your new layout, you can either print it, or you can save it to the master pages to use it as a template again.

To save it as a master page from the cog pop-up menu, navigate to **Save Page | As New Document Master**.

 If you choose the other option, **To Document Master**, you will write over the existing template of your theme.

There are a lot of options in the book module when editing layouts, so much in fact that you could probably fill a whole book on just that one topic. You can add multiple images and multiple textboxes to the page, and you can even add a map. The cog pop-up menu contains options for aligning the text and photo boxes, and for setting the photo boxes to preset the aspect ratios.

Printing your page

Once you are ready to print, simply select **Print** from the file menu, or press *command* + *P*. This will bring up the print dialog for printing books.

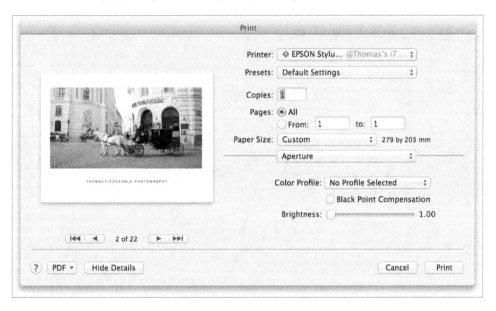

Here you can click through a preview of the pages. If you have only used one of the pages of your template, but the others are still blank, be sure to set the page that is to be printed to the correct range, otherwise your printer will output a lot of blank pages.

Ordering prints using Apple's print service

If you don't have a printer, but still want to get prints made from your processed images, there are several options open to you. You can export your images to a USB key and bring them to a local print shop, or you can use an online print provider, or thirdly, you can use Apple's own print ordering service.

There are a couple of limitations to using Apple's print service. First of all, it is not supported in every country. Secondly, you will need to have an Apple ID with a credit card associated with it. If you bought Aperture through the Mac App Store, you have probably already fulfilled the second requirement. Thirdly, the sizes of print you can order vary from country to country, so if you are hoping to get a large print, the option may not be available in your region and you may have to use a third-party service.

To order a print or prints from Apple's service, first select the image or images you want to order, and from the menu, navigate to **File | Order Prints**.

This will bring you to the **Sign In** screen. Here you will see what options are available in your country, enter your Apple ID, and sign in.

Once you sign in, you will see a list of your images and the sizes available. Enter the number of prints you want of each size. If you are ordering prints for a large number of images, and you have quite a long list, then having to do this manually can be a bit of a chore. Fortunately, you can use the **Quick Order** function at the top of the print order dialog box to set the number of prints you want to order. To use the **Quick Order** function, select the size you want from the pop-up menu. Then click on the up and down arrows to control the number of prints, at the selected size you want to order for all your images.

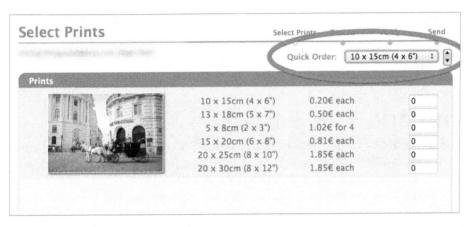

Once you have selected all the sizes you want, just follow the rest of the instructions. Your prints will then upload to Apple's servers and your prints will arrive in the mail in a few days (or weeks, depending on where you live).

Ordering prints from a third-party service

If you would prefer to order prints from a third-party service (or if Apple does not support your country), you will more than likely have to do it manually. There are a couple of things to be aware of when prepping your images for export that can save you time and money.

Export your images at the maximum quality possible. Many services will have limitations on the size and the file format of images that they will accept (although these limitations are not as severe as they once were). Most will accept JPEG and so you should set up an export preset to export a JPEG at 100 percent quality. Some labs will accept TIFF, so if you want, you can use the TIFF format. This may preserve better color, depending on the printing process, but in all likelihood, a full quality JPEG is probably good enough.

Check with your printing service what color space or color profile they want their image in. If you are using a consumer lab, you should use the sRGB profile, but if you are using a professional lab they may prefer Adobe RGB, or another profile. Check with the lab before ordering. A professional lab should also be able to provide you with a color profile for proofing.

Always order a small selection of test prints from a lab before ordering a large number of prints, or before ordering for a client. It is better to sort out any issues on a small order, rather than have a large order that is not printed properly.

Make sure your images resolution can support the size of the image you are ordering. This is especially important when ordering poster prints. There is high debate over what megapixel is required for what sized prints, but be aware that your images may appear soft if they are not of a high enough resolution. Most online services will warn you if your image is not of a high enough resolution for your chosen print size.

Summary

In this chapter, we covered numerous tips and advices for getting better prints from Aperture. Hopefully, by now, you have a good grasp of what is possible to get out of Aperture by printing or by ordering prints. As we have covered, Aperture's print dialog is surprisingly complex, and there are a few traps that can trip you up if you are not careful.

We also looked at how to create virtual prints by using the print dialog to print to a PDF file. We looked at how this can be useful when creating contact sheets to e-mail to clients. We also looked at how to use Aperture's powerful hidden page layout engine that is hidden in the book module, to create more advanced print layouts, and we looked at ordering prints from either Apple's print service, or from a third-party service.

If you have been reading through this book from start to finish, you should now have a better understanding of the whole Aperture workflow. While this book didn't cover every button and menu item, we looked at lots of techniques and tips for extending your Aperture skill set, so that you have a good working knowledge of how to get the most from the software.

It was my goal throughout this book to not just teach you how to do a task, but also the thinking behind it, and by giving you a little bit of knowledge and understanding of how Aperture works in a given situation, you can better approach the software. I wanted to show you how I work with Aperture, and to share the lessons I have learned over the years. Sometimes a cold formulaic instruction book can be just that, cold and formulaic. Hopefully by sharing the experience of using Aperture for several years, you have gained an insight into how an experienced user uses Aperture, and you can see the software from a different perspective.

Index

Thank you for buying
Mastering Apple Aperture

About Packt Publishing

Packt, pronounced 'packed', published its first book "*Mastering phpMyAdmin for Effective MySQL Management*" in April 2004 and subsequently continued to specialize in publishing highly focused books on specific technologies and solutions.

Our books and publications share the experiences of your fellow IT professionals in adapting and customizing today's systems, applications, and frameworks. Our solution based books give you the knowledge and power to customize the software and technologies you're using to get the job done. Packt books are more specific and less general than the IT books you have seen in the past. Our unique business model allows us to bring you more focused information, giving you more of what you need to know, and less of what you don't.

Packt is a modern, yet unique publishing company, which focuses on producing quality, cutting-edge books for communities of developers, administrators, and newbies alike. For more information, please visit our website: www.packtpub.com.

Writing for Packt

We welcome all inquiries from people who are interested in authoring. Book proposals should be sent to author@packtpub.com. If your book idea is still at an early stage and you would like to discuss it first before writing a formal book proposal, contact us; one of our commissioning editors will get in touch with you.

We're not just looking for published authors; if you have strong technical skills but no writing experience, our experienced editors can help you develop a writing career, or simply get some additional reward for your expertise.

Apple Motion 5 Cookbook

ISBN: 978-1-849693-80-6 Paperback: 416 pages

Over 110 recipes to build simple and complex motion graphics in the blink of an eye

1. Easy to follow, hands-on instructions that simplify the learning process

2. Lots of in-depth information for FCPX users looking to integrate more motion graphics into their projects

3. Learn keyboard shortcuts that will save you hours and navigate Motion's interface like an expert

Kinect in Motion – Audio and Visual Tracking by Example

ISBN: 978-1-849697-18-7 Paperback: 112 pages

A fast-paced, practical guide including examples, clear instructions, and details for building your own multimodal user interface

1. Step-by-step examples on how to master the essential features of Kinect technology

2. Fully-functioning code samples ready to expand and adjust to your need

3. Compact and handy reference on how to adopt a multimodal user interface in your application

Please check **www.PacktPub.com** for information on our titles

Multimedia Programming with Pure Data

ISBN: 978-1-782164-64-7   Paperback: 350 pages

A comprehensive guide for digital artists for creating rich interactive multimedia applications using Pure Data

1. Carefully organized topics for interactive multimedia professional practice

2. Detailed reference to a large collection of resources in the open source communities to enhance the Pure Data software

3. Visual explanation and step-by-step tutorials with practical and creative multimedia applications

Augmented Reality with Kinect

ISBN: 978-1-849694-38-4   Paperback: 122 pages

Develop your own handsfree and attarctive augmented reality applications with Microsoft Kinect

1. Understand all major Kinect API features including image streaming, skeleton tracking and face tracking

2. Understand the Kinect APIs with the help of small examples

3. Develop a comparatively complete Fruit Ninja game using Kinect and augmented Reality techniques

Please check **www.PacktPub.com** for information on our titles